J. D. SALINGER'S
THE CATCHER IN THE RYE

J. D. SALINGER'S
THE CATCHER IN THE RYE

A Cultural History

Josef Benson

ROWMAN & LITTLEFIELD
Lanham • Boulder • New York • London

Published by Rowman & Littlefield
A wholly owned subsidiary of The Rowman & Littlefield Publishing Group, Inc.
4501 Forbes Boulevard, Suite 200, Lanham, Maryland 20706
www.rowman.com

Unit A, Whitacre Mews, 26-34 Stannary Street, London SE11 4AB

British Library Cataloguing in Publication Information Available

Library of Congress Cataloging-in-Publication Data

Names: Benson, Josef, 1974– author.
Title: J. D. Salinger's The catcher in the rye : a cultural history / Josef Benson.
Description: Lanham, Maryland : Rowman & Littlefield, 2018. | Includes bibliographical references
    and index.
Identifiers: LCCN 2017035350 (print) | LCCN 2017036600 (ebook) | ISBN 9781442277953 (elec-
    tronic) | ISBN 9781442277946 (hardback : alk. paper)
Subjects: LCSH: Salinger, J. D. (Jerome David), 1919–2010. Catcher in the rye. | Caulfield, Holden
    (Fictitious character)
Classification: LCC PS3537.A426 (ebook) | LCC PS3537.A426 C3216 2018 (print) | DDC 813/.54—
    dc23
LC record available at https://lccn.loc.gov/2017035350

♾ ™ The paper used in this publication meets the minimum requirements of
American National Standard for Information Sciences Permanence of Paper for
Printed Library Materials, ANSI/NISO Z39.48-1992.

Printed in the United States of America

For my wife, Brenda,
whose central advice for this book was
"Just tell a story. People love stories."

CONTENTS

ACKNOWLEDGMENTS

Many thanks to Stephen Ryan for offering the project to me. Thanks to my friend and editor Bob Batchelor for his editorial vision and grit. Thanks to my colleagues Tara Pedersen and Teresa Coronado for their input at the very beginning. Thanks to Jay McRoy for the many casual discussions and laughs that helped form the structure of the book.

INTRODUCTION

In 1991, when I was sixteen years old and living in Springfield, Missouri, my mother gave me *The Catcher in the Rye* for Easter, along with Thoreau's *Walden*. The books stuck out of a large Easter basket, jutting from green shredded plastic grass as though they had grown out of that synthetic ground like carrots. I was the same age as J. D. Salinger's iconic protagonist Holden Caulfield, and my mom must have figured that Holden and Thoreau were better role models than Jim Morrison. I had recently quit playing football and baseball and discovered marijuana and the Doors. My hair was longer, and I'd put on a little weight. *The Catcher in the Rye* revealed to me that contrary to what my English teachers had told me in grade school and high school, writing was not about following rules. Reading the novel for the first time demonstrated to me that writing could actually be truthful. Hanging out with Holden for those two hundred or so pages temporarily satisfied a hunger for a point of view that was not about following rules and sparked a lust in me to tell my own truth.

Throughout high school, *Catcher* became a touchstone for my friends and me as well as a sort of litmus test for other people. If people had read the book, then they were cool; if not then they likely weren't. This counted for girls as well. I often introduced myself to new people as Holden, sometimes Holden Caulfield, just to see if they would recognize the name. Over the years I have come to realize that my experience was actually pretty common among first-time readers of the novel. I loaned my small white copy to each member of our circle of friends, and before long our gang developed a sort of literary reputation that was undeserved and stemmed mostly from our casual references to Holden, Salinger, Stradlater, and Ackley. I read several other books around that time, including *The Great Gatsby*, *The Adventures of Huckleberry Finn*, *The Old Man and the Sea*, and *On the Road*.

My first job during my sophomore year of high school was as an usher in a movie theater. I would stand behind a sort of podium with a slot in it for torn tickets and read. The ticket podium functioned nicely as a sort of lectern. As moviegoers approached me with their tickets, I would sometimes leave them standing there as I read to the end of a paragraph or otherwise found a convenient place to stop and mark my place.

Eighty-five years earlier, in Springfield, Missouri, a mob formed in the town square after two masked men attacked a man and a woman in a buggy. The man was beaten unconscious and the woman was raped. The man identified two particular black men as the perpetrators despite the fact that the attackers had worn masks and the woman stated positively that neither man had been her rapist. Soon both men were jailed anyway, and once word got out in town that two black men had raped a white woman, a lynch mob formed at the jailhouse. Both wrongly accused black men were hanged, and their bodies were burned in the town square. The mob returned to the jail later that night and hanged another black man who had been charged with an unrelated murder. This act of racial terrorism instigated a mass exodus of black people from Springfield, Missouri. Even today, one rarely sees a black person in Springfield.

One weekday afternoon in the summer of 1991, a white man approached me with his ticket and noticed that I was reading *The Adventures of Huckleberry Finn*. "That book should be banned," he said.

"Really? Why do you say that?"

"Cause it has the word *nigger*."

I told the man that I thought it was probably a pretty accurate depiction of its usage during the time. The man snorted and asked me whether I was one of those college kids. I told him I was in high school. He then gave me his ticket. I tore it and gave it back to him, and as he walked by me he loudly farted.

I found this sort of reaction disgusting but also empowering and exciting. Finally, I had found something that struck fear in the hearts of people that was not inherently childish. I realized books were weapons that some folks found intimidating. I realized the knowledge one gleaned from books had power and that an intellectual youth was downright terrifying. More specifically, I had found something in the complexities of race that I felt was absolutely true and at the same time deliciously dangerous.

My dad is an educator and writer, and when I was in kindergarten in Des Moines, Iowa, before I moved to Springfield with my mother, step-father, and sister, he enrolled me in a magnet school for diversity. There were only two or three other white kids in the whole class. The rest were black, Latino, and Vietnamese. I remember being particularly fond of the Vietnamese boys who barely spoke English and would get pulled out of class for extra language instruction. This early kindergarten experience certainly had a hand in my easy realization as a high school student that our culture was misguided in relation to how we think about race. Very early on I understood that the very concept of race was inaccurate, that the black and Vietnamese kids with whom I attended kindergarten were my classmates and friends, not members of other races.

The natural realization that white supremacy was real and at the same time totally ridiculous galvanized me intellectually largely because of the intensity of the reactions that I received from other people when I talked about race. Around this time I also read *The Portable Nietzsche* and decided that I agreed with the rock-star philosopher that there was no God. I also found the whole idea of marriage laughable, perhaps because I had recently witnessed my father getting married for the second time. I was attracted to ideas that shook the status quo, provided that I truly believed in them.

My friends and I got high and drunk and argued about religion, racism, and marriage. Looking back, I'm pretty sure that I instigated these discussions and single-handedly influenced the tenor of these small get-togethers. Despite my excitement in relation to espousing viewpoints that many found troubling, I was a long way from being truly "woke." *The Catcher in the Rye* models attitude without activism, style without substance, and this defined my style of critical thinking to that point.

I remember going gay bashing my junior year with a bunch of upper-classmen at a park in Springfield that was rumored to be a gay cruising zone not far from the town square where the three black men were murdered by a mob of white people more than eight decades earlier. I wasn't even sure what I was looking for as I ran into the night with the other boys bent on some sort of symbolic violence. I'm not even sure that we were searching for other human beings as much as proving to one another that we were prepared to root something out in ourselves. Some of the guys had baseball bats and were sprinting through the empty park howling. No one told us what we were looking for, and the only thing we found was emptiness.

The following year was the first presidential election in which I could vote. It was 1992, and Slick Willy was up against Bush 41. I didn't vote.

Soon a lot of people began talking about college. I hadn't the slightest idea where I was going to go to college or how to go about it. I was barely attending my high school classes, and many of my friends had already dropped out and started working and getting their own apartments. I told everyone that I was applying to several schools even though I hadn't even started. Ironically, I was reading a ton and writing poems and stories, but I failed to make the connection between what I was doing and college.

One morning I was in my bedroom at my mother's house nursing a terrible hangover, and a navy recruiter called me and encouraged me to join. I knew that my dad had been in the navy and that several writers I admired had served in one capacity or another. Four months later I was flying to San Diego for navy boot camp.

In the navy, my identity as a writer became fully fleshed out if not completely earned. As I did in high school, I recruited several of my shipmates and fashioned together a sort of band of poets and writers. We read Rimbaud, Wilde, Ginsberg, and Burroughs and talked a lot about sexuality. In the early nineties the navy had not yet fully integrated women. There were a few women in air squadrons who would come aboard when we were deployed, but for the most part our regular ship's crew was made up primarily of men, more than five thousand of them. Sexuality became an exciting topic to discuss, like racism, marriage, and God, and yet there was something slightly more dangerous in this subject if only because the threshold was closer and more accessible. This was when Clinton's "Don't Ask, Don't Tell" policy was in effect, and it seemed like questions about homosexuality in the military were on everyone's mind. We also knew about the stereotypes regarding sexuality and sailors. Homosexuality was another sort of dangerous topic that excited me intellectually. When one of my best friends' father died and we were up very late drinking and he was crying, I held him and kissed the back of his neck.

I was honorably discharged from the United States Navy in the summer of 1995. The following spring I matriculated at Missouri State University in Springfield, Missouri. Not long after that, I declared my major as English and my minor as philosophy. I graduated in 2000 and went on to earn a master's degree and Ph.D. at the University of South Florida. Then in 2013 I found myself interviewing for an assistant professor of literature and creative writing job at the University of Wisconsin, Parkside, where I would be slated to teach, among other courses, African American literature and courses in women's, gender, and sexuality studies.

One could say this journey began while reading *The Catcher in the Rye* and figuring out that one could be rebellious in a way that was empowering, instead of acting out in a way that buried one or landed one in rehab or jail. One question that I had to answer in my interview for the UW Parkside job and that I have had to answer several times in my career as an academic was in relation to teaching African American literature as a white man and women's and gender studies as a straight man. The question has been worded in several different ways by students and faculty alike, but the gist is basically the following: Where do you get off teaching African American literature as a white man or gender studies as a straight man? My answer to that question has evolved over the years. The first part of my answer has to do with the assumptions hidden in the question. The assumptions are that I am white and straight. While anyone who looks at me would assume that I am white or Caucasian and very likely straight, when filling out any sort of legal form, for example, I do not claim whiteness. If there were a box for straight, I would not check that, either. Whiteness and straightness are fictions of which I want no part. Whiteness and straightness are social constructions that have been historically used to exclude people designated as nonwhite and nonnormative, whether they are Irish, Italians, Latinos, of African descent, or members of the LGBTQ community. Whiteness and straightness are ideas that I want to abolish.

The second part of my answer is that antiracist "white" or "straight" intellectuals are nothing new. Historically there have been many white, presumably straight, men, who have devoted their professional lives and sometimes their actual lives for antiracist causes and popular struggles of all kinds, men like John Brown and William Lloyd Garrison. Further, the discipline of whiteness studies and gender studies, so often maligned in the press, have produced terrific scholars such as Steve Martinot, George Lipsitz, Noel Ignatiev, and Michael Kimmel. These men are race-changers and progressives who have coupled their antiwhite, antisexist ideologies with political agendas, who have betrayed the white race and abandoned rigid social hierarchies in favor of strengthening the human race. Reading Salinger's *The Catcher in the Rye* empowered me to think critically about my culture, but it did not empower me to act. This is the central reason for the book's sustained vilification as well as its popularity.

This is a book about a book, a cultural biography of an artifact. Julie Rivkin and Michael Ryan note that prior to the sixties and seventies, *culture* either referred specifically to artistic pursuits and production or more broadly among anthropologists to ritualized social behavior.[1] In terms of the former, artistic production often reflects and affirms the culture in which it arises. Visual art and music frequently underscore the values of the people who produce and consume it. However, cultural artifacts can also be at odds with a community or social order and function as a means of resistance to a dominant ideology. The story of *The Catcher in the Rye* began with the author, J. D. Salinger. As the creator of the artifact, his life before and after publication informed the story of the novel. Once the novel was released into the world, the book took on a narrative of its own somewhat independent of the author. The author no longer had total control of the book and its life as it moved through time and touched readers who in turn changed the narrative and historical direction of the novel. This lack of control over his work haunted Salinger for the rest of his life. After publication, the reading public and the United States also became characters in the story of the novel. As the writer of this book, I am also a character in the story of the novel that has zigged and zagged through the culture perhaps more dramatically than any other book in U.S. history.

As a cultural artifact, *The Catcher in the Rye* has both functioned as a means of resistance to a dominant white power structure and as a tool of domination. Holden slams the social hierarchy of which he is a part. The only problem is that he slams it to a shrink. Otherwise he keeps it inside. This central structure of the novel reflects the story of the artifact as it has lived through the decades. Its author, its readers, and its hero are closeted; thus the book's potential as a means of resistance was never actually realized.

The overriding argument in this book, alongside its cultural history, has to do with the extent to which closetedness has been a part of the

American culture and a part of the story of the book. Salinger was a privileged upper-class, half-Jewish New Yorker who wrote the first half of *The Catcher in the Rye* just before liberating the Nazi concentration camps, and then wrote the rest of the book right after. This is the most important fact about the novel because this event is the reason why Holden rails against his culture and detests aggressive male behavior. Salinger witnessed the result of male white supremacist aggression in Nazi Germany and saw its likeness rampant in the United States.

In the book, Holden rails against the institutionalized white supremacist culture ensconced in his prep school, Pencey, and embodied in a whole host of aggressive men whom he cannot stand. That his rant is actually being related to a psychiatrist suggests that Holden until that point has not really come out of the closet as a Jew or as a man dissatisfied with his culture. His sympathy for the downtrodden informs his troubled feelings about Antolini and Carl Luce, as well as a man whom he sees through a hotel window don women's clothing, including white stockings, pumps, bra, corset, and a black evening dress. Holden longs to be a catcher in the rye, the kind of person who helps people who need it the most. The problem is that his desire never gets beyond the interior. There is no reason to believe that Holden will be any different after his sessions with the doctor. Holden's views essentially remain in the closet, and this is his appeal for a massive reading public spanning more than six decades, as well as the reason the book has been feared and banned decade after decade.

At a time when anti-Semitism was waning, if only because Jew hating was no longer in vogue, Holden's closeted Jewishness, coupled with his diatribe against whiteness, presents an opportunity for Holden to be a sort of race-changer, a man who appears to be part of the in group or dominant culture but who is actually part of the out group and who uses his insider status to undermine the dominant culture and draw attention to its venal status as social construction. In addition to Holden Caulfield being in the closet throughout the novel, Salinger represents perhaps the most reclusive and closeted author the world has ever known. The impetus for his reclusiveness in part stems from his lifelong attachment to very young girls as well as, if to a lesser degree, his reported lack of a testicle. Salinger's fear of being held accountable for his sexual exploits involving very young girls is a pervasive theme throughout his work and throughout his life. Like Holden, Salinger never made good on his potential to be a true change agent or transcendent progressive figure. Instead, he opted to shun the world and become more famous for his disavowal of other human beings than for his desire to be anyone's catcher in the rye.

The popularity of the novel over the decades in part has to do with Holden's and Salinger's brand of activism: interiority with no clear political agenda. Holden and Salinger add their two cents, Holden to a shrink, without any real sacrifice. Neither has any skin in the game and neither make any real sacrifices. It is all talk and anticipates a nation of slacktivism. On the other hand, the novel has been one of the most widely censored and banned books because of its *potential* for change. As I say in the book, the novel is about the closet but it is also about the door.

In the decades since the *Catcher in the Rye* appeared, there have been many instances of potential race-changers who like Holden Caulfield failed to emerge from their cultural and racial closets, famous figures who were heavily influenced by nonwhite cultures but who failed to parlay that influence into any sort of racial program. These are white men who had an opportunity to betray their race in order to better the human race. These are decade-defining symbolic contextualizing figures who have existed in relation to whiteness, some as betrayers, some as opportunist black exploiters, and one a black figure unable or unwilling to escape whiteness. I compare all these men decade by decade to Holden and Salinger as would-be betrayers of whiteness who in most cases wound up being upholders of white supremacy and oftentimes masculine straightness as well.

Chapter 1 argues that Salinger's half-Jewishness and his exposure to the gruesomeness enacted on Jews in the Nazi concentration camps inform Holden Caulfield's rejection of upper-class white privilege. Because Salinger wrote much of the book while engaged in a brutal war against an enemy whose goal was to genocidally rid the world of Jews, the novel is replete with racial dynamics and concerns. As an adolescent, Holden struggles to embrace an alternative to traditional aggressive maleness, at times criticizing behavior that he also imitates. The likelihood of Holden achieving his goal of becoming a catcher in the rye or agent of change rests on his ability to navigate the racial, sexual, and gendered minefields of a culture that predisposes men to be oppressors.

Chapter 2 discusses the decade of the fifties in relation to Salinger, Elvis Presley, and the novel. Both Salinger and Elvis began the decade as potential race-changers, white insiders and racialized outsiders, whose work spoke to their liminal positionings. By the end of the decade, Salinger had retreated to his compound in Cornish and into a religion that stressed sexual restraint despite already courting and eventually seducing a fourteen-year-old girl and after that a sixteen-year-old girl whom he eventually married. Like Salinger, Elvis retreated back into his whiteness, emblematized by his Graceland mansion in Whitehaven.

Chapter 3 notes that not only did Salinger quit publishing at the midway point of the sixties, but he also turned down several opportunities to engage publicly in ongoing discourses concerning racial equality in the United States. As a result of his silence and the disavowal of his readership, he more than his work became the most legible cultural artifact available to the public within the Salinger machine. Salinger's refusal to join the many cultural movements in the sixties despite his growing wealth and fame highlights not only the potential of the decade but also perhaps why many of these potentialities eventually sputtered. The Altamont Free Rock Festival headlined by the Rolling Stones at which a black man was murdered underscored the cost of cultural leaders abdicating their privileged roles as vanguards.

Chapter 4 contends that while Salinger was making romantic advances toward eighteen-year-old girls, dodging fans of his work, and criminalizing his readership, men like William Kunstler were displaying how one goes about betraying one's race and privilege in favor of the human race. This chapter discusses the novel and its author in the 1970s and the Attica prison uprising and activist white lawyer William Kunstler, who for a brief time embodied a revolutionary race-changer who overcame his preconceived racist notions about black prisoners at Attica, put his life on the line, and represented the imprisoned black men who demanded more humane prison conditions. Kunstler coupled activism with critical thinking and subsequently demonstrated his racial agency during the uprising, only to witness the negotiations fall apart and the National Guard storm the prison and murder dozens of people, including other National Guardsmen. Salinger, on the other hand, spent the better part of the decade running from a public who refused to accept the author's silence.

Chapter 5 discusses the parallel lawsuits in the eighties between Salinger and his would-be biographer Ian Hamilton and Vanilla Ice and Suge Knight, as well as three murderous devotees of the novel and their unexpected link with the author and the novel's protagonist. The chapter offers that the decade of the eighties solidified Salinger as a closeted hero, like his protagonist Holden Caulfield, willing to legally defend his right to his closet to the bitter end even if it meant destroying the careers of other writers. To the reading public, Salinger and Holden were characters that were highly admirable for their inaction. Analogously, what Vanilla Ice illustrated in the decade of the eighties in his legal fight with producer Suge Knight over his hit rap album *To the Extreme* was that crossing over, of coming out of the closet as a race-changer, can be a messy business with disastrous effects when the crossover is not accompanied by an active political agenda that challenges whiteness or the status quo in general. What Salinger in the 1980s further reminded us was that the author's inability to emerge as a true catcher in the rye was still informed by his fear of being targeted as a pervert.

Chapter 6 maintains that the legacy of Salinger and *The Catcher in the Rye* wound up having more to do with the author's silence than anything the man ever wrote. His presence within the popular culture in the last twenty-five years in movies and on television has almost always been in relation to his reclusiveness, which has obscured the anti-establishment, anti-white message in his work. The last twenty-five years have also presented the American culture with two presidents in Bill Clinton and Barack Obama, whose racial legacies are still being debated.

Culturally we are not done grappling with *The Catcher in the Rye* or Salinger. Since 2015, three major stage and film productions based on Salinger and *The Catcher in the Rye* have surfaced. *Holden*, an off-Broadway play written and directed by Anisa George, premiered in 2015 in New York and then enjoyed another run in January 2017. The film *Coming through the Rye* came out in 2015, and the movie *Rebel in the Rye* was released in September 2017. This book in part attempts to explain why it is that our fascination with the man and the novel continues year after year and decade after decade.

I

THE BIRTH OF A NOVEL

Holden Caulfield and J. D. Salinger: Two Men in the Closet (a Close Reading)

You never really get the smell of burning flesh out of your nose entirely, no matter how long you live.—J. D. Salinger[1]

That J. D. Salinger was a privileged, upper-class, half-Jewish New Yorker who wrote the first six chapters of *The Catcher in the Rye* just before witnessing the horrific results of racial prejudice in the Nazi concentration camps, and then wrote the rest of the book right after, represents the single most important fact about the novel. These experiences underscored what Salinger already knew, that his own Jewishness exposed him to the same forces behind the Holocaust, since, at best, Jews in America were conditionally white, provided they assimilated and defended existing hierarchical divisions.

In the spring of 1945, as a member of counterintelligence, Salinger was one of the first Americans to liberate the Nazi concentration camps and witness the horrors of the Holocaust that included piles and piles of still burning and smoking bodies. These human beings were murdered due to fraudulent notions of race that also applied to Salinger, namely, that the Jew represented an inferior race of subhumans that had infected the German body, caused Germany's defeat in World War I, and required eradication.

The particular camp that Salinger liberated was Kaufering IV or the *Krankenlager* (camp for the ill). Designated for the sick, the camp actually functioned as an extermination camp since the afflicted prisoners were simply left to die. When the Nazis realized that the Americans were about to liberate the camps, they burned alive masses of prisoners. The prisoners whom Salinger encountered, both dead and alive, represented the weakest and most helpless among the mostly Jewish inmates. These were human beings considered unworthy of life by virtue of their Jewishness. Though Salinger never published anything about his experiences specifically, according to David Shields and Shane Salerno, one of the unpublished works that Salinger completed presumably after 1965 and locked in a safe revolved around diary entries from a counterintelligence officer during World War II that culminates in the liberation of a concentration camp. When Salinger and other counterintelligence officers and soldiers first entered the camp, they likely had their guard down. There was no way they could have expected what they saw. Infiltrating the camps was supposed to be a positive experience, something heroic. Nothing prepared Salinger for the hell in which he found himself upon entering the camp. Nearly two hundred prisoners had been recently killed in all manner of atrocity, and the liberating soldiers found mass graves containing thousands more. There was also evidence of attempted but failed escapes as several inmates were found hacked to death by bloody axes near railroad cars in which the SS were likely trying to transport them before the Allied forces arrived.[2] The soldiers also found stacks of bodies wherein some people were still alive and blinking, the weight of other humans crushing them. Many of the soldiers immediately broke down and wept minutes after entering the camp.

Salinger's own half-Jewish ancestry surely compounded the profoundly devastating experience of seeing the utter dehumanization and loss of life that day. Had he been born in Germany, Salinger very well could have been one of the prisoners who were either burning, among the stacks, or so thoroughly broken that they could not even look another man in the eye for fear of being killed. Salinger bearing witness to these thoroughly desperate human beings cast a pathos-laden die that would eventually emerge in his doppelganger Holden, who demonstrates throughout the novel an almost innate compassion for the powerless. Salinger's half-Jewishness and his personal exposure to the gruesomeness enacted on Jews in the Nazi concentration camps inform Holden Caulfield's struggle and ultimate rejection of upper-class white privilege in *The Catcher in the Rye*. In the novel, Holden encounters what Salinger encountered in the war: the absurdity and deathly destruction inherent in acquiescing to racial, sexual, and gendered hierarchical divisions to which he is also vulnerable.

About a year earlier, Salinger, as a member of the Twelfth Infantry Regiment, was a part of the second wave in the D-day assault, the surprise Allied invasion of Germany that set the stage for the liberation of Germany from Nazi control. He was twenty-five years old and most of his fellow soldiers were around nineteen or twenty. By the end of June, Salinger's regiment had lost two thousand out of three thousand men. At first Salinger was very excited and proud to be contributing to the war effort, but as the bodies began to stack up, his enthusiasm quickly waned until he wanted nothing to do with the war at all. As a member of the counterintelligence, Salinger's duties included, among other things, interrogating Nazis and supporting the regimental ground pounders. Salinger and three other men would often arrive in certain towns before the regiment in order to get the lay of the land and scope out any potential dangers. While all this was going on, Salinger was writing stories and sending them to publishers as well as working on his first novel that would turn out to be *The Catcher in the Rye* and make him a very reluctant celebrity, a fate that would dog him for the rest of his life. In order to get a suspected Nazi to talk, one typical strategy Salinger and the other members of counterintelligence used was forcing the man to dig his own grave.

According to his buddies, Salinger would often write wherever he could, including on the side of the road. The only photograph of him working on *The Catcher in the Rye* shows him at a wooden desk that looks like it was set up in the middle of the forest. Salinger is sitting at the table smoking a cigarette over several sheets of paper lying on the desk and looking at the camera as though it was a nuisance, a prescient picture indeed.

Perhaps the worst battle that Salinger and his regiment encountered was the Battle of Hürtgen Forest. About fifty square miles, the forest sat along the German and Belgian border. Just beyond it was the Rhine, which the American forces designated as an important strategic point requiring driving the Germans out of the forest. The Germans' primary defensive strategy was using artillery to explode in the treetops, causing deadly shards of wood to come raining down on the Allied forces. Seven thousand men were lost in four weeks, more than thirty thousand all told. It was a disastrous defeat for the Allied forces.

In the winter of 1944, Hitler decided to wage one last battle with everything he had, more than two hundred thousand German soldiers. The battle would become known as the Battle of the Bulge and go down in history as perhaps the largest battle in American history abroad. More than a million soldiers were involved. It was Hitler's last-ditch attempt to gain control of the war, his greatest gamble. At this point in the war, many of the German soldiers were children whom Hitler had deliberately raised for this purpose, some as young as fifteen. The idea that Salinger inevitably witnessed German soldiers sixteen years of age gruesomely dying on the battlefield, some of whom he may have killed himself, casts his sixteen-year-old protagonist in an eerie light. Perhaps this was where his innocence was shattered, where the threshold of childhood stopped. After the initial assault, the Allied forces regrouped and overwhelmed Hitler's undertrained forces. Salinger's regiment was given a Presidential Unit Citation for their role.

Despite Salinger's mother not being born Jewish and converting once she married Salinger's Jewish dad, and the fact that according to strict Orthodox Judaism only a person whose mother is Jewish can be Jewish, Salinger was very much raised in a Jewish household and considered himself Jewish. He had his Bar Mitzvah when he was thirteen[3] and very likely had the H classification as part of his serial number engraved on his dog tags in the army that identified him as Hebrew or Jewish. The idea that one's mother's blood is more important that one's father's blood in Orthodox Judaism calls attention to the limitations of the blood metaphor of racial purity and the general fluidity of racial distinctions. The Nazis had an extremely complicated system in place with regard to how they treated half Jews. Some were spared the concentration camps at least initially, but all were discriminated against to one degree or another and eventually, had the war not ended, all would have certainly been murdered. On the other hand, there were many instances where someone was marked as a Jew and sent to the concentration camps regardless of religion or ancestry. In other words, one was a Jew if the Nazis said so, and "blood" had very little if anything to do with it.

Jewish soldiers like Salinger fought against an enemy whose murderous ethos was in part shared by a large swath of the population in the

United States. Salinger was aware of U.S. prejudice against Jews and, for example, hated the Ivy League because of its overt anti-Semitism. On several occasions, Salinger discussed his appreciation that his alma mater Ursinus College was not an Ivy League school and therefore not a hotbed for anti-Semitism and hate.

Salinger only attended Ursinus for one semester in 1938. He wrote for the student newspaper, including a feature called "J.D.S.'s The Skipped Diploma" wherein columns appeared concerning random observations or sometimes scathing movie reviews. Ursinus now offers a scholarship in Salinger's honor that proffers the winner thirty thousand dollars toward the over-forty-thousand-dollar tuition. The recipient also gets to stay in Salinger's dorm room for a year. Just outside the door is a plaque commemorating the author's onetime presence. The scholarship specifically recognizes promise in creative writing and goes to writers who demonstrate unusual and offbeat talent and a voice not unlike Holden Caulfield. [4]

In the novel, Holden relates that he would rather die than attend an Ivy League school and comments that Ivy Leaguers all look alike. Salinger was very aware of the open prejudice and discrimination rampant in Ivy League schools. For example, he knew that these schools limited the number of Jews they would accept. Further, the Ivy League represented the locus of the U.S. eugenics studies movement, a movement driven by the notion that procreation of poor people and minorities needed to be stifled. This area of study that flourished in the United States before World War II ultimately informed the Nazi genocidal movement.

Salinger's Jewishness may have even delayed the publication of *The Catcher in the Rye*. After liking and expressing interest in Salinger's novel, Harcourt, Brace editor Robert Giroux passed it along to his boss Eugene Reynal, a Harvard- and Oxford-educated man with a reputation as a terrific snob and exactly the kind of man Salinger loathed. [5] Reynal predictably did not like the book and consequently missed out on one of the all-time best sellers.

Initially Salinger's agent submitted the manuscript to the *New Yorker*, which promptly rejected it because they believed Holden was too unbelievable as a character, way too articulate for a sixteen-year-old. After Harcourt, Brace rejected it—likely on the grounds of Salinger's Jewishness—Salinger took the book to Little, Brown. Not long after, Harcourt would also pass on Jack Kerouac's *On the Road*.

Little, Brown accepted Salinger's only novel but soon realized they were dealing with an unusual author. Salinger refused to send out advanced copies of the novel, ordered Little, Brown not to send him any reviews (positive or negative), and refused to do any publicity for the book. Michael Mitchell came up with the cover for the book, a wild carousel horse, and Salinger loved it. The image referenced the end of the book when Holden meets up with Phoebe in Central Park at the carousel, often described as a positive ending to a rather dreary, negative book. In retrospect, considering Salinger's penchant for writing about children with well-developed libidos and his, to say the least, questionable history with young women, sometimes as young as fourteen, the image of the carousel assumes a sinister quality, since carousels are spaces often filled with children.

Because of his Jewishness, Salinger's racial status in the United States was murky despite his upper-class whiteness. His membership into the "white race" was tenuous and probationary and there was little to ensure that he would not be persecuted in his own country once he returned from the war. The Jew in the United States prior to World War II was conditionally white, provided that he was willing to uphold male-centered white supremacist hierarchies. The U.S. government and its citizens at one time or another were uncertain whether Jews, Catholics, Germans, and Irish were white, highlighting racial whiteness as a fluid notion often employed expediently for economic or political gain by those in power.

The cultural fabrication of race, including the "Hebrew race," fuels Holden Caulfield's disillusionment with his own privileged "white" culture. His closeted Jewishness compels him to continually identify with the downtrodden, the excluded, and the underprivileged in New York in the late 1940s.

The notion of racial Jewishness still persisted in the 1940s. An *Atlantic Monthly* article titled "The Jewish Problem in America" claimed that the Jews had become Europeanized only by virtue of their placement in the United States. Journals like the *Baltimore Sun* and *Detroit Free Press* referenced without qualification the Nazis' attempts to solve their racial problem.[6] U.S. Jews, like people of color, were once considered visibly Jewish and were discriminated against based on this difference. As early as the nineteenth century, Jews were considered black. Holden Caulfield struggles to align himself with upper-class white male privilege because his Jewishness compels him to identify with difference.

Because of skin color and facial characteristics, Jews were literally seen as black.[7] The otherness of the Jew reached its peak in the Nazi concentration camps in World War II. The extermination of Jews in Nazi Germany during the Second World War was predicated on the racial otherness of the Jew. Ironically, though, once the world found out about the horrors of the extermination camps and the fate of the Jews, among others, in Nazi Germany, American Jews became less othered and less racialized in the United States since racializing Jews was part of a Nazi ethos villainized in the United States. While it was no longer fashionable to be overtly anti-Semitic in the United States for fear of being *like a Nazi*, anti-Semitism still existed in the hearts and minds of many, and Jews like Salinger were still vulnerable to discrimination and worse. Like the Irish and Italian before, the pallor of the Jew did not literally lighten, even though like the Irish and the Italian before, the Jew became less black within a racial symbolic wherein those in power were white and those who were not were black, or *of color*. That the Jew and Zionism in general is now the darling of the U.S. neoconservative movement has more to do with the blackness of Muslims and Islamophobia than with the whiteness of the Jew.

Salinger never made it a secret that Holden was a stand-in for himself, and on several occasions via letters admitted that Holden Caulfield was based on himself when young. There are parallels in the book between Holden's characterization and Salinger's own life. For example, Salinger and Holden are both six feet two and a half; both at one point managed a fencing team and lost the team's equipment on the train; both tend to be loners; Salinger's family lived in the same general area of New York City where the Caulfields reside; and both Salinger and Holden were kicked out of school.

The technique of autobiographical fiction reflects Salinger's admiration of Ernest Hemingway, a fiction writer who famously wrote about his own life and employed first-person narrators similar to himself. Salinger was an unabashed fan of Hemingway and loved the way he wrote. Aside from the details of characterization, the similarities of author and narrator in *The Catcher in the Rye* run even deeper, particularly in relation to war and religion.

Salinger wrote much of the novel while he was embroiled in some of the most brutal combat any U.S. soldier has ever gone through: "Salinger's division was in combat longer than any other division in the European theater. He saw the worst fighting you could possibly see, maybe, in the entire Second World War. Anyone who lived through this level of fierce combat this long would have been profoundly affected."[8] Some argue that the inevitable result of participating in a war for an extended period of time is certain insanity that requires therapy and no doubt leaves terrific psychological scars. War imagery and allusions to religion pepper the novel. The specter of war is never far from Holden, whether he is pretending that he is shot or rejecting war outright. For a chunk of the novel, Holden pretends that he is gut-shot and barely keeping his entrails from falling onto the floor. Holden's wounds stem from Salinger's war experiences, especially at Kaufering IV. Salinger hid his terrible war wounds and the resultant disillusionment with his own privilege by imputing it to Holden, who admits that he is hiding the wound.

There is ample evidence of Holden's preoccupation with religion and desire to keep his own religious background, a background similar to the author's, a secret. He makes it clear that he is Catholic and expresses annoyance that people are always trying to figure out his religion. Salinger changed the religions of Holden's parents to reflect the exact opposite of his own. In fact, Salinger's father, Solomon Salinger, was a Jew from Chicago. He met and married Marie Jillich, a Catholic, and she changed her name to Miriam.[9] In the novel, Holden says that his parents are different religions. Holden never mentions what religion his mother is, but it is safe to assume that she is a Jew; thus, Holden's father reflects the conversion of Salinger's mother, and according to Orthodox Judaism, Salinger chose to make his protagonist a full Jew by giving him a Jewish-born mother. That Salinger chose to have Holden's mother be a born Jew instead of his father and then sort of hide it within the novel speaks to his conflicted relationship with his own religion. On one hand, he felt it important that Holden be fully Jewish according to Orthodox Judaism, but on the other hand he wanted this idea codified and masked.

Holden is preoccupied with religion and gets annoyed when he feels that anyone is trying to determine his. He is a character who is in the closet about his own Jewishness. That Jewishness does not play a larger role in the novel points more to its conspicuous omission rather than to its lack of importance; it is the omission itself that lends Holden's religion significance since the omission points to the existence of a secret hidden within a closet.

Holden can barely disguise his lack of reverence for Christianity. He makes a point of acknowledging Jesus when discussing atheism so as not to betray his Jewishness. Holden's reluctance to outright reject Jesus stems from his Jewish insecurity.

Salinger's experiences in the war left him a broken man disillusioned with his own country. His only solace was reassembling himself in disguise as Holden Caulfield, an upper-class closet Jew who sees the blatant hypocrisy rampant in U.S. culture.

In 1945, not long after liberating Kaufering, Salinger, armed with the first six chapters of what would later be *The Catcher in the Rye*, checked into a Nuremberg psychiatric hospital. Despite earning five battle stars and a Unit Citation for Valor, Salinger was a thoroughly broken man. Likely his battle fatigue was less from actual battle than from his experiences at the *Krankenlager*. Salinger spent two weeks at the hospital and while there wrote a letter to Hemingway in which he praised the author and asked whether things would get better once he got out of the army and some time had passed. He also mentioned that he was working on a very sensitive novel that was certainly *The Catcher in the Rye*. Salinger's disillusionment and sobering epiphanies stemming from his war experiences explain Holden's difficulties in coming of age in a country predicated on phony racial, gendered, and sexual divisions.

The idea of Holden being in the closet about his religion assumes the idea that the closet can refer to anyone with a secret in relation to his or her identity. The closet functions as a self-imposed limitation to actualization based on the fear of being found out as anything less than normal, and the result can be devastating, not only for the person whose identity is a secret but also for the concomitant collective closet that results. The closet prevents political power, stifles voices, and caters to hate and discrimination. The drive to be normal keeps people silent. With regard to *The Catcher in the Rye*, Holden's religious isolation and fear of being outed as a Jew is one of many closets that Holden inhabits. The book can then be read in part as Holden's failed attempt to emerge from the various closets in which he dwells.

As a closet Jew, Holden is both white insider and racialized outsider. Holden's white privilege is predicated on whiteness purporting to be a single monolithic consciousness, opposed to one that is fragmented or doubled. Holden tenuously masks his double consciousness as racial Jew and upper-class white and consequently identifies with marginalized identities, including those existing on sexual borderlands. One can define white male privilege as the internal false denial of double consciousness and sexual borderlands.

Holden is uncomfortable with his fraudulent privilege. The primary result of Holden's masked and divided consciousness is his interrogation and ultimate rejection of white privilege. Holden intuits the unfairness of venal white culture and criticizes those who cultivate, profit, or blindly accept it. His most intense criticisms are leveled at Pencey Prep, a stand-in for the primary institution for inculcating white entitlement and privilege in prospective white leaders. The Pencey Prep brand is reflected in images of young men playing polo, the pinnacle of romanticized and privileged white culture: cultivated wealth with the promise of power and prestige. The implicit message in this picture is that these men represent the elite and everyone else does not matter. Holden understands that the men playing polo are symbolic of his future, even though secretly he cannot identify with this promise because of his Jewishness. Holden's otherness prevents him from feeling the same sort of blind elitism as the fictitious men in the picture. To him, the polo game is clearly rigged. When his history teacher, Mr. Spencer, tells him that life is a game that one needs to play according to the rules, Holden considers but does not say that he thinks life is a game for the privileged only, and that for those who are not privileged there is no game at all. Importantly, Holden only thinks this rejoinder when he is with Spencer but assumingly only actually articulates it to the shrink to whom he is telling the story. The line for Holden between where all the hotshots are and the other side is blurry at best. His unwillingness to accept his privileged status despite his Jewishness, and perhaps embrace anti-Semitism or some other prejudice endemic to white guy culture, is the central reason why *The Catcher in the Rye* is the most iconoclastic book of all time. Holden undermines important institutions for aspiring white power brokers such as Pencey Prep. Here is the locus of inculcating elitism by which many are judged and found lacking. Here is the locus whereby the white heterosexual male configures himself as the rightful standard bearer entitled to the highest echelons of society. To him, the system is cruel and promotes exclusion. At best, what Holden can hope for is a job like his father has as a corporate lawyer, but what he really wants is a place out in the country with a woman he loves, something Salinger attempted to have his entire life.

Holden's self-reliant anticapitalist idealism causes him to lament anything that compromises this, including his own contributions to class elitism. For the white power structure, the scariest thing about *The Catcher in the Rye* is that readers identify with Holden and sympathize with his criticisms of fundamental American capitalistic values. Holden's identification with and sensitivity to the neglected and underprivileged manifests in his concern for the ducks in Central Park. Privileged New Yorkers do not spend their time thinking about where the ducks in Central Park go for winter, just as they do not generally concern themselves with the homeless or underprivileged. People simply do not consider the ducks. Even if they do, perhaps they just assume someone will take care of them over the winter. Holden knows better than to assume the powerless will be taken care of because Salinger knows better, having witnessed firsthand what happens to the powerless when no one is paying attention. When Holden asks Horowitz, a Jewish taxi driver, where the ducks go in the winter, Horowitz becomes irritated and then outraged that Holden is asking this question; perhaps as a fellow Jew he thinks it is ridiculous for Holden to worry about the ducks when a Jew already has plenty to worry about. For Horowitz, the ducks should act like the fish, or the Jew, and just accept cold reality and live right in the ice.

Holden's preference for Native Americans to Christopher Columbus in the Natural History Museum further reflects his identification with the powerless instead of the historical white power structure. Holden admires the Native Americans whom Columbus massacred more than the conquering Spaniard. The source of Holden's sadness and interest in humanity is the sorrow and pain Salinger bore after seeing the inmates in the Nazi concentration camps. The novel is a testimonial, a witnessing. Thusly, Holden Caulfield's deeper dream of becoming the catcher in the rye stems not only from a desire to protect children from falling off a cliff and landing in phony adulthood but also to safeguard the oppressed.

The death of James Castle in the novel represents an important nexus between Salinger and Holden in relation to the deadly consequences of a culture predicated on exclusion and hate. Holden suggests that James Castle was possibly raped for standing up to his bullying tormentors and as a consequence jumped out of his dorm window to his death on the concrete below where Holden sees him. Holden notes that Castle is actually wearing Holden's turtleneck sweater that he had loaned him. Holden admits to seeing Castle's body torn apart on the pavement. Like Salinger,

Holden must *witness* the cruel barbarism and death that results from a society where men violently vie for power by invoking cultural divisions based on race, gender, and sexuality. That Castle is wearing Holden's sweater suggests Holden's identification with the dead boy. It could have easily been him lying there just like it could have easily been Salinger in the concentration camps.

Like Huck Finn in Mark Twain's *The Adventures of Huckleberry Finn*, Holden Caulfield decries hypocritical and destructive prevailing social realities tied to race, gender, and sexuality, due in part to his closeted Jewishness, ironically causing him to question his own moral character and sanity. Further, Salinger's indictment of male-centered white supremacy through his narrator Holden Caulfield largely explains the vehement conservative criticism of the novel that resulted in *The Catcher in the Rye* representing not only one of the most loved books of all time but also one of the most feared and banned.

The similarities between Mark Twain's *The Adventures of Huckleberry Finn* and Salinger's *The Catcher in the Rye*, and the reason why both books have so often been banned, center on each narrator's personal evolution in rejecting white privilege. The one difference is that Huck's rejection results in a political act while Holden's results in a trip to the analyst. Huck decides to free Jim despite the pressure he feels from his community to abide by and maintain racial power structures. In breaking the law for a higher moral cause, Huck ironically surrenders to his own wickedness and immorality and abandons his privilege as an aspiring white man. In *The Catcher in the Rye*, Holden feels at times perverted, crazy, and troubled for not categorically rejecting queer sexualities and because of his reluctance to seduce and even sexually assault women, both typical characteristics of mainstream guy culture. Mark Twain delineates Huck's inability to embrace a racial politics contrary to his experience with Jim and illustrates how Huck decides that if freeing Jim means that Huck is wicked and will go to hell, then so be it. By illustrating the unjustness of condemning a man based on artificial divisions and socially constructed valuations based on race, Huck's moral choices indict white power structures in the same way that Holden's indict mainstream guy culture. These character choices and transparent rationalizations invite empathy that in turn moves the reader to side with the narrator against the prevailing white culture. The internal monologues of the two narratives effectively transmit the underpinnings of their iconoclastic actions to the reader and, in most cases, cultivate reader sympathy. While Twain's *The Adventures of Huckleberry Finn* primarily focuses on racial injustice, Salinger's *The Catcher in the Rye* highlights the intersections of race, sexuality, and gender. Racial hierarchies depend on male heterosexual privilege to maintain static power structures by promoting further divisions among the ranks of men and women. By subjugating white women, for example, the white power structure ensures white men's exclusive access to white women's bodies and unlimited access to all women's bodies, a hallmark of white supremacy. Further, by controlling white women, white men can control a white woman's power to corrupt the fraudulent metaphor of blood purity through miscegenation.

Holden's reluctance to categorically reject Mr. Antolini for his fairly obvious sexual advance indicates Holden's development as a human being, his potential rejection of power structures, and his sensitivity toward marginalized identities due to his own closeted Jewishness. That Antolini is drunk, references Holden's handsomeness, and touches Holden when he only has his underwear on, suggests Antolini's homosexual desire. Because Antolini admits to *admiring* Holden and then evinces some concern with keeping his actions from his wife after Holden startles, the older man's sexual desire of the much younger Holden is hard to miss. The more salient point is that Holden ultimately is willing to see beyond it and later the next day considers going back to Antolini's apartment. Similar to the way Huck has been taught to treat black people and especially slaves as inferior human beings, Holden has been taught to violently respond to alternative sexualities, particularly anything that resembles an advance. Like Huck, though, Holden's actual interactions with Antolini prevent him from doing so, marking a positive evolution in his human development and another rejection of white privilege. Holden is sensitive to the potentially powerless because of his own tenuous white identity. He finds it difficult to dismiss anyone based on artificial divisions based on race, gender, or sexuality since he knows that he could also be dismissed due to his hidden racialized status as a Jew and because the author understands the dire consequences of racial persecution.

The second example of Holden rejecting mainstream guy culture centers on his refusal to objectify and even rape women. Perhaps the most important aspect of a white male dominant society is maintaining the disempowerment of women primarily through sexualization and dehumanization. Sexualizing and objectifying women even by rape reasserts male dominance and negates a woman's autonomy and power to self-actualize. Rape is the physical manifestation of a social order that casts women as objects for the pleasure and control of men. Under this strain, women struggle to compete with men in arenas of power, because to men, women are always already dehumanized via their sexualization. Further, women alone have the power to undermine the fraudulent metaphor of blood purity by engaging in miscegenation. They arrive to the game already under the yoke. Misogyny and sexual violence have become synonymous with mainstream guy culture. Holden feels less than a man because he sees the value and humanity in women. Salinger through Holden underscores a white power structure wherein basic human decency in relation to heterosexual relationships is considered weak. Salinger suggests that Holden feels his refusal to exploit women actually undermines his ability to engage in healthy sexual relationships. Holden's refusal to dismiss Antolini for his sexual advance and his refusal to sexually exploit women mark him as a potential traitor to a white male culture that has only provisionally accepted him to begin with.

The Adventures of Huckleberry Finn and The Catcher in the Rye represent two of the most iconic and influential American novels ever written, and both novels have origins that complicate the idea that they are monolithically white novels. The Catcher in the Rye was written by a man whose whiteness was probationary at best and one hundred years earlier would have been denied. As earlier noted, the Jew in the nineteenth century was considered black. Further, Salinger's experiences in World War II, namely, his witnessing of the horrors of exclusionary whiteness, compels his narrator Holden to lash out at white institutions that inculcate exclusionary whiteness.

Shelley Fishkin makes a compelling case that the most notable aspect of Huck Finn, Huck's voice, was actually based on the vernacular of a young black boy. The most salient and memorable aspect of Huck Finn is his dynamic use of language, and as Fishkin reveals, that voice is actually African American.[10] The idea that Huck's style of speaking is decidedly black complicates the history of American literature and at the very least undermines the idea that American literature can with any coherence be separated by fraudulent notions of race or contrived racial dichotomies such as black and white. Famously, Ernest Hemingway declared that all of modern American literature started with Huckleberry Finn, and William Faulkner once referred to Twain as the patriarch of American literature. These declarations would suggest that American literature it-self as we know it is racially unknowable.

The primary reason why *The Catcher in the Rye* represents one of the most frequently censored books across the country over the last seven decades revolves around Holden's rejection of white mainstream guy culture. Not coincidentally, the folks at the root of the banning of the novel have almost always identified themselves as members of the "Mo-ral Majority" or the New Right. This New Right is primarily composed of fundamental white male Christians. Racial whiteness initially depended on whether non-English whites were considered fit to self-govern and depended on the willingness of non-English whites to buy into racial whiteness to the detriment of whichever groups at the time were not considered white.

Holden's rejection of whiteness despite his Jewishness compromises his right to whiteness according to the primarily white male heterosexual Christians who most fear the effect of the novel on readers. Consequent-ly, Salinger's novel has been condemned as un-American by primarily white Christian groups.

For example, in the fall of 1977, the Reverend Paul W. Hornung of the First Baptist Church of Elmer, New Jersey, wrote an open letter that was printed in the *Elmer Times* that called for the immediate removal of *The Catcher in the Rye* from the curriculum at Pittsburgh Township High School. In the letter, Hornung referred to the novel as garbage and called on the board to implement a screening committee for all required reading at the high school in order to preserve the community. Hornung admitted he had not actually read the whole book but that he had been shown passages and found them pornographic. Likely Hornung was shown the passages by Ruby and John Rauser, whose daughter brought the book home from school one day. Ruby then read the book and found it totally depraved and profane. John also found the book filthy and the two de-manded that the board ban the book. [11]

The following month the board met in a small municipal courtroom and set up fifty chairs that were mostly full of the townspeople eager to learn the fate of the novel many so desperately wanted to censor. Four-teen speakers offered their thoughts, including John Rauser who read excerpts from the novel. Ruby at one point referred to the book as sex education. When all fourteen speakers finished, some in favor of retain-ing the novel for fear of going down the slippery slope of censorship, the board was silent for a full two minutes, no one offering to make the necessary motion to vote on whether to ban the book at all. Ruby quickly announced that every member should say their name aloud so to have a record of their failure to act. The book was ultimately retained since no one on the board moved to vote on the book, and their silence, as it was interpreted, was essentially a vote to keep the novel in the school. [12]

Another example of Holden's disavowal of upper-class privileged white culture is his use of slang. Holden's language reflects his rebel position and has often represented low-hanging fruit for critics of the book who are not honest about their true fears. The true nature of much of the criticism of Salinger's only published novel and its long history as a controversial and often banned text lies in its rejection of the white power structure helmed by wealthy, Christian, white, heterosexual men, a group Holden mercilessly derides in the novel.

In his short story "Blue Melody," published in 1948, just three years before *The Catcher in the Rye*, Salinger highlights the devastation of racial persecution not in Nazi Germany but rather in the southern United States, suggesting his awareness of the connection between the two countries and forecasting the same theme coursing through *The Catcher in the Rye*. The story evidences Salinger's preoccupation with racial themes and concern for marginalized nonwhites vulnerable to the white power structure in the United States.

In this story, a first-person narrator while stationed in Germany in 1944 relates a story he hears from a fellow soldier named Rudford on the way to the German front. Rudford hails from Tennessee and the story he tells revolves around two kids, one of them being him, and their relationship with a jazz pianist named Black Charles who generously plays for the children whenever they ask him to. The story is set in the Jim Crow South and illustrates the lethal effects of internalized racism.

Though the children adore Black Charles and love to hear him play the piano and to hear his niece Lida sing, they are completely unaware of the risks they impose on Black Charles, whose café sits on the wrong part of town. The children treat Black Charles like a toy, and ultimately their ignorance of the social forces at play in the community cause the death of Lida.

Despite Rudford's book learning, he is seemingly unaware of segregation and the idea that in Agersburg white-only hospitals will not admit black people even in life-and-death situations. When Lida's appendix bursts, Rudford orders Black Charles to take the girl to two white hospitals only to be denied admittance. As a result, Lida dies and Rudford is partially to blame, compelling him to pursue a career in medicine and right the wrongs of his youth in the war.

The narrator in "Blue Melody" assures readers that the story is not a slam on the South but makes it clear that Rudford has a southern accent and hails from the South. The implication in this statement has an ironic effect. The narrator pointing out that the story is not a knock on the South has the reverse effect, causing the reader to assume that the story *is* about the South. The story takes place in Agersburg, Tennessee, a town, according to Rudford, that still celebrates southerners who fought to maintain slavery, so much so that they named a street for a woman who killed five Union soldiers.

The story that Rudford relates to the reader and the fact that the two men are heading to the German front in World War II highlights the shared racial element of American segregation and the Holocaust. One year after the events of the story, the actual author, J. D. Salinger, would liberate the concentration camps.

The point of the story is that Rudford has decided to become a medic in the war, a war deeply entwined with and driven by racism, because of his experiences as a youth. Rudford feels in some ways responsible for the death of Lida Louise because of his ignorance about the rampant racism in his hometown.

Rudford is a boy with a lot of book smarts largely because his father forced him to read textbooks that he had written. Rudford's father abandoned his salesman career in Boston when he met and married a rich girl in Agersburg. Once his wife died giving birth to Rudford, Rudford's father bought a publishing company and published his own books. The important aspect of these details is that the father forced Rudford to read his books at a very young age and as a result Rudford knows many things found in books. Salinger goes on to note that there were also important things Rudford learns as a young man that could not be found in his father's books, namely, lessons involving art, love, and eventually the perils of racism.

Black Charles's café sits on the wrong side of town, off limits to the white children. When Rudford first invites his classmate Peggy to hear Black Charles play at the café, Peggy tells Rudford she is not allowed on the street on which Black Charles's café sits.

The other important point to make here is that Salinger presents children who are more mature and advanced than most children, similar to Seymour and Buddy in *Hapworth 16, 1924* and Esmé in "For Esmé— with Love and Squalor." There is a sort of sinister current running through the story in relation to these eleven-year-old children hanging around with a much older man in Black Charles that will be echoed in *The Catcher in the Rye* in the relationship between Holden and Antolini and that was echoed in Salinger's own life.

It never occurs to Rudford that he is putting Black Charles in a very precarious situation by coming to his place in the middle of the day and spending so much time with him in general. It is as though the racial aspect of the relationship or age difference between Charles and the children never occurs to Rudford, suggesting that despite his book learning he is very naïve to the social realities of Agersburg.

The children go so far as to punch Black Charles in order to get him to get up and dutifully play for them. According to Rudford, Black Charles never chastised the children for hitting him or forcing him to play when he was trying to sleep. Instead, Rudford suggests that Black Charles was always all too eager to satisfy the whims of the children, not unlike false depictions of slaves whistling and generally enjoying themselves in the fields.

Despite seeming completely naïve, the children are also depicted as precocious. And when they request a particular song for Lida to sing, Lida responds by questioning the appropriateness of such a song for kids. Unbeknownst to the kids, Black Charles risks backlash from the town folks who may not think it appropriate for two young children, especially a young girl, to be spending time with a much older black man in a bar on the wrong side of town.

Rudford's and Peggy's careless treatment of Black Charles and Lida culminates in Lida's death. Before Rudford goes away to boarding school, perhaps as a punishment imposed by his father for spending too much time on the wrong side of the tracks, Rudford, Peggy, Black Charles, Lida, and Lida's mother get together for a picnic. When Lida's appendix ruptures, Rudford immediately takes charge of the situation, barking orders at Black Charles even though he is far younger than Black Charles and not even a blood relative of Lida's. Rudford first hears Lida cry out while he is lying on his back in the grass. It is telling that he is able to see cotton in the southern sky without associating it with slavery.

Ostensibly, due to the books that he has read, Rudford knows right away that Lida has a burst appendix. In this instance, his book learning is on point, but his street smarts and awareness of the social structures in Agersburg are lacking as they are for most white people who do not have to ever think about race. When Rudford demands that Black Charles take Lida to Good Samaritan Hospital, Black Charles knows that Lida will not be admitted to the white-only hospital and yet defers to the younger Rudford. Here again Rudford displays an indifference to Black Charles's feelings and simply expects him to do whatever Rudford says, likely because Rudford is white and Black Charles is black and Rudford is used to black people doing whatever white people say, including children, such as forcing Black Charles to play the piano for the children whenever they beckon him.

Once they arrive at the hospital, Rudford once again barks orders at Black Charles. Rudford punches Black Charles, reminiscent of a slave master violently forcing with impunity a slave to act. Salinger under-scores the idea that Rudford is performing the role of slave master to Charles's role as slave and that even when his beloved niece's life is on the line and Charles realizes the lethal repercussions of Rudford's ignor-ant error, Charles feels compelled to obey. It is clear that Rudford and Peggy are not Charles's best friends but rather two white kids who enjoy a social power over Charles that he is powerless to avoid.

Notably, the entrance to the hospital is a great white entrance, symbol-izing the fact that the hospital is a white-only Jim Crow–segregated hos-pital. Rudford thinks that he is taking charge of the situation and becomes frustrated with what he thinks is Black Charles's laziness and general stupidity. When Lida is not admitted because she is black, Rudford must confront the limits of his book learning. The kids experience similar treatment at another white hospital and soon Lida is dead.

At the beginning of the story, it is clear that Rudford is a medic in the army. The implication is that Rudford's experience with Lida impelled him to become a doctor. The idea that his role in the army during World War II when the Nazis were exterminating the Jews is that being a medi-cal professional dovetails with the notion that his formative experience in Agersburg, when he was confronted with a prejudice that cost the life of someone who he cared about very much, had a profound effect.

For Rudford, the death of Lida was the most important event of his young life. At the end of the story, Rudford runs into Peggy, whom he has not seen since Lida's death. This occurrence is interesting in that during the story Rudford's relationship with Peggy is inspired by Lida's singing. After her death, the two are never able to recover the romance of their young relationship.

Lida's death has caused Rudford to devote his life to helping people since he could not help Lida when she needed him most. His stupidity and internalized racism aided in her death. Rudford has put it all behind him. There is a good chance that he will be among the soldiers the following year who liberate the concentration camps. This time he will be ready. Perhaps he will even be a catcher in the rye.

Salinger's short story "Blue Melody," published just three years before his only novel, instantiates Salinger's concern for racial themes in the United States likely driven by his experiences in the war and anticipates Holden's antiwhite sentiments.

Salinger was honorably discharged from the army on November 22, 1945. Instead of returning to the States, he signed up for a new tour of duty that involved hunting down Nazis. That he would choose to stay in the country despite his mental anguish suggests Salinger's commitment to rooting out the Nazi white supremacist ethos. His job was to ferret out any remaining Nazis or Nazi collaborators. One of the women he likely interviewed was a German named Sylvia Welter. The two would marry later that year, but Salinger would try to keep it a secret since there were laws against American soldiers marrying German women. While Sylvia was not officially a member of the Nazi Party, many odd facts in her life suggest that she was likely a Nazi Gestapo informant. For example, over a four-year period she was enrolled at six universities. This was consistent with the Nazi practice of employing attractive young females to spy on students and faculty. As a result of the spying and informing and the information gathered by many of these informants, many students and professors were executed, especially members of the student movement.

The following year the two left Europe for the States, but after only a few weeks in the States Salinger bought Sylvia a plane ticket back to Europe. The annulment papers filed by Salinger and his father's lawyer cite bad intentions and misrepresentations on the part of Sylvia. Many close to Salinger felt that Salinger found out about her job for the Gestapo and this was the reason why he sent her packing. The fact that after witnessing the horrors at the *Krankenlager* Salinger promptly married a Nazi is nothing short of mind boggling. Sylvia was in her early twenties when she allegedly worked for the Gestapo. Perhaps this experience led Salinger to seek out women purer than Sylvia, untouched by age and far younger than two decades. Over the years Salinger claimed that Sylvia had bewitched him and that the two communicated telepathically and visited one another in their dreams. Not long after his divorce, Salinger began dating a fourteen-year-old girl and then not long after that married a girl whom he had met when she was sixteen and immersed himself in the Vedanta religion, which preaches, among other things, sexual restraint.

Few novels have been written under more duress than *The Catcher in the Rye*. Salinger wrote much of the book while in the heat of some of the worst military battles of all time. He was present during the invasion of Normandy, the Battle of Hürtgen Forest, the Battle of the Bulge, and most importantly, the initial liberations of Nazi concentration camps. As a Jew what he saw had a tremendous effect on his view of the United States and its own scourge of racial discrimination. No longer could he accept his place among elite whites and contribute to a power structure that played a significant role in the Holocaust. Holden Caulfield represents this development in Salinger and explains Holden's inability to exist within institutions that socialize white male students into privileged men who maintain racial, sexual, and gendered divisions in order to perpetuate their own privileged status. The real value of the novel and the reason why it, along with *The Adventures of Huckleberry Finn*, represents one of the most feared and banned books of all time is that it depicts not only Holden's physical rejection and disavowal of white culture and Pencey Prep, but also the intellectual machinations of his disavowal. Readers are privy and sympathetic to Holden's thoughts and feelings in relation to a brutal uncompassionate culture predicated on fraudulent and destructive human divisions based on social constructions of race, gender, and sexuality. The conservative fear of the book lies in Holden's magnanimity, his desire to protect the marginalized, the left out, the less fortunate, the left behind, and the readers who love him, who want to hang out with him, who identify with him, and who want to be him.

Holden's goal once he leaves Pencey Prep late Saturday night is to get away as fast as he can and lie low in New York before going home Wednesday to face his parents. His money runs out by Monday, but what concerns him most over the weekend revolves around what he thinks happened between Stradlater and Jane Gallagher on their date that Saturday night. Holden fears that Stradlater may have aggressively seduced or even raped Jane, a girl who Holden thinks may have already been the victim of sexual violence and for whom he cares a great deal. Holden's obsession with what happened between Stradlater and Jane on their date in Coach Banky's car reflects Holden's deep hostility toward Pencey's entitled white male sports culture and his moral drive to be the catcher in the rye for the powerless and marginalized. For Holden, phoniness among men equates an exaggerated macho male performance endemic to athletes and tough guys. Throughout the novel, Holden criticizes exaggerated maleness while at times simultaneously aping it. Just as Holden hides his religion in a metaphorical closet, so, too, does he hide his distaste for macho behavior and his sympathy for what he describes as perversity, or behavior different from the accepted male behavior at Pencey Prep. His failure to fully disavow macho maleness and embrace difference ultimately prevents him from realizing his dream of becoming a true change agent or catcher in the rye. Holden often describes himself as crazy, mad, perverse, severely wounded, terminally ill, or generally on the verge of death. These feelings of abnormality, inadequacy, and deep affliction stem from his inability or lack of desire to successfully perform a brand of exaggerated macho maleness marked by sexual aggression as well as his incapacity to also distance himself from it. Holden's self-diagnosed sexual inadequacy and perversity may also stem from Salinger's testicular deformity that he hid throughout his life, as well as his lifelong taboo sexual preference for adolescent girls. Holden despises exaggerated male behavior and cites his dead brother Allie as a positive alternative marked by intelligence, sensitivity, and vulnerability. *The Catcher in the Rye* is very much an indictment of traditional and destructive exaggerated male behavior that flourishes in a rape culture that also fears and marginalizes diverse sexualities. That the narrative structure of the novel revolves around Holden coming out of the closet about his hostility toward macho behavior and sympathy toward diverse sexualities, does not necessarily suggest that Holden is on the path toward a healthy gender identity. What is more likely is that Holden himself will be diagnosed as a pervert and ushered deeper into the closet, a space the author wound up occupying for most of his life.

Holden's preoccupation with sex and his concern about his hormones or his fears that he is becoming a homosexual may have its origins in Salinger's own documented fear that having one testicle somehow predisposed him to effeminacy. Evidently Salinger lied about this anatomical anomaly that initially kept him out of the military, saying, "Because of a slight heart ailment, he was 'classified I-B with all the other cripples and faggets [*sic*].'" According to Shields and Salerno:

> The I-B classification was given to those fit for only limited military service. "Cripples and faggets [*sic*]" is enormously telling of Salinger's self-assessment, because the "slight heart condition" was almost certainly a convenient fiction to disguise the existence of a congenital deformity. While researching Salinger's second meeting with Hemingway . . . we discovered an unreported detail about Salinger's physical condition. . . . Salinger [told] Hemingway "that he didn't think the army would take him . . . [because] he had only one testicle." . . . Hemingway told Salinger, "Those doctors were such fool[s]. With a touch of the finger, they could have put your other testicle down."[13]

Salinger seeking advice from Ernest Hemingway with regard to Salinger's self-assessed literal male anatomical lack strikes one as particularly interesting considering Hemingway's position as macho standard bearer among American writers. Salinger's relationship with Hemingway echoes Holden's relationship with Stradlater; Salinger admired Hemingway and went out of his way to meet the man on more than one occasion. Salinger even defended Hemingway against charges of the man's destructive masculinity, but much of Salinger's worldview changed after his experiences in World War II, including his assessment of Hemingway, who Salinger may have felt expressed the wrong message when it came to a man needing to demonstrate his courage under fire. Likewise in the novel, Holden at first seems to tolerate and even respect and admire Stradlater but soon turns on him and attacks him because of his exaggerated masculinity and date with Jane.

According to one report, during the war Hemingway visited Salinger's regiment, and the two along with a few of Salinger's buddies were shooting the breeze about which was the better pistol, the German Luger or the U.S. Colt .45. Hemingway felt the Luger was superior and to illustrate his point unholstered his own Luger and shot the head off a chicken. Salinger was not impressed.[14]

Salinger's missing or undescended testicle may have been a bigger deal to him his entire life than one might expect. Shields and Salerno note, "Two women independently confirmed that Salinger had this physical deformity, about which, one of them said, he was 'incredibly embarrassed and frustrated.'"[15] Shields and Salerno also speculate that fear of his deformity being made public may have been one of the many reasons why he avoided the media throughout his life.[16] Notably in *Franny and Zooey*, one of the characters conflates masculinity with one's testicles.

The other aspect of Salinger's life that may be responsible for Holden's sympathy with nonnormative sexualities and his fear of becoming a homosexual has to do with Salinger's reported interest in young girls.

Many critics have noted Salinger's penchant for writing about children in his fiction. That Salinger clearly preferred younger women and likely felt self-conscious about it renders the character who is most like him, Holden Caulfield, sympathetic with other sorts of so-called perversions.

Salinger's reported sexual preference for young women can be described as hebephilia, sexual attraction to persons between eleven and fourteen years old.[17] There has been some disagreement as to whether hebephilia ought to be listed in the manual of mental disorders. As women have gained more rights and agency and with the advent of feminism, instances of older men marrying or otherwise having sexual relationships with young women has declined since more value has been put on women gaining an education rather than simply having children. The desire to include it as a mental disorder likely caused Salinger to also consider it something to hide and of which to be ashamed. Further, in seducing young girls, Salinger perpetuated a culture of male dominance that his novel and protagonist seem to repudiate. As Salinger proved to have a conflicted relationship with his religion, so, too, did he have a conflicted relationship with his sexuality; both conflicts are heavily represented in his only novel.

Salinger's struggle with his sexual preferences shows up in several of his stories, such as "A Perfect Day for Bananafish" and "For Esmé—with Love and Squalor." In the lead story of Salinger's *Nine Stories*, just before he kills himself, Seymour Glass meets a very young girl on the beach whose mother has left her alone to play. Seymour describes his own new wife to the young girl as terribly superficial and materialistic. He then proceeds to go swimming with the little girl and at one point kisses her foot. Directly after this scene, he walks up to his hotel room and shoots himself in the head.

In "For Esmé—with Love and Squalor," a soldier stationed in France happens upon a church in which children are singing in a choir. One of the choir members—again, a little girl—catches the narrator's eye, and later he meets her in a café and what follows is very similar to a budding love story. This time it is the young girl who is the forward one. The narrator admits to the young girl that he has been lonely. After the two have a little talk, which seems like a flirtation between two adults, the narrator relates to the reader that he left the café upset and confused.

The second half of the story depicts a mental breakdown by the narrator that ostensibly is caused by the war but, juxtaposed with the first half of the story, may be in regard to his frustrating interest in girls far younger than he. The narrator of the first half points out a quote suggesting that hell is the inability to love. It is reasonable to suggest that the quote is in relation to the narrator's inability to love young children for whom he feels so much because of social mores. Ultimately the man is comforted by a letter from the little girl.

These are two of Salinger's most famous stories, and in both, the main characters can be viewed as struggling with their romantic and sexual feelings toward children. In both cases, the characters experience mental breakdowns after intimate exchanges with young girls. Given that Salinger himself had a pattern of behavior similar to this and for which it seems logical that he felt guilty, it would stand to reason that this was a problem for him that he considered nonnormative if not unnatural.

In *Hapworth 16, 1924*, a novella that first appeared in the *New Yorker* and then later in the unauthorized *The Complete Uncollected Short Stories Volume 2*, Salinger depicts the seven-year-old narrator Seymour Glass as possessing a highly developed libido. The bulk of the novella consists of a letter that Seymour has written to his parents from summer camp. The most interesting aspect of the letter centers on Seymour's crush on a camp nurse. Despite Seymour's awareness that he is too young to be sexually active, he nevertheless insists on his precocious libido. At another point in the letter, Seymour beseeches his siblings not to hide behind their youth. It seems as though Seymour, or Salinger, makes an argument as to the possibility of sexually developed children and perhaps thusly creates a safety valve for his own sexual preferences.

In *Raise High the Roof Beam, Carpenters and Seymour: An Introduction*, Salinger laments the idea that readers may try to diagnose or otherwise apprehend some flaw in writers whom they admire, especially one of a sexual nature.

It is difficult not to read these clues from other works by Salinger in light of Salinger's history with adolescent girls. The dynamic seems to appear time and time again in all his works, and the author at times appears to be defending himself against would-be attackers and doctors who might be eager to diagnose him as a pervert or criminal. Another interesting and perhaps mere coincidence is that the name of the town where Pencey Prep is located in *The Catcher in the Rye* is Agerstown. In Salinger's important story about race relations in the United States, "Blue Melody," featuring a close relationship between two children and a grown black man, the town where the action takes place is named Agersburg. The prefix *ager* refers to age, how old someone is, and is most common in the word *teenagers*. Could Salinger have been codifying his obsessions?

In Daytona Beach in early 1949 at the Sheraton Hotel, a war-jangled Salinger happened upon a fourteen-year-old girl reading *Wuthering Heights* and struck up a conversation with her about the book. During the conversation, Salinger told the girl that he was a writer and that he had published a few stories in the *New Yorker* and seemed proud of that fact. The girl was Jean Miller, and she remembered that Salinger had grimaced when she told him that she was fourteen. He told her that first day that he was thirty years old and for the next ten days the two met up and took walks together down the beach and ate ice cream and fed the seagulls. Miller reminisced that she felt as though he was escorting her. She noted that she thought he might have been deaf in one ear from the war and that these moments on the beach gave him respite from his anxiety. She said she thought he was attracted to her innocence. According to Miller, Salinger was the first adult who seemed to actually care what she had to say. She was also very aware that he was extremely handsome. The Daytona Sheraton was the site of Salinger's breakup with Sylvia Welter three years earlier and would be the site of his breakup with another young girl—Joyce Maynard—twenty-three years later in 1972.

Over those several days at Daytona Beach with Jean Miller, Salinger discussed the novel that he was working on, *The Catcher in the Rye*. He told her that he was mostly nervous about how people would receive the novel. Miller also remembered that Salinger talked a lot about child actors like Judy Garland in *The Wizard of Oz*. She said he liked the innocence of childhood before self-consciousness set in. On the last day, he told her that he would like to kiss her good-bye but that he could not. According to Miller, her parents did not approve of their relationship, and even though Salinger wrote Jean close to sixty letters that first year, many of them were thrown out. Miller's father accused Salinger of only being after one thing. Over the next four years, the two would meet at Salinger's place in Cornish and in New York and send lots of letters to one another. Miller noted that Salinger was very upset about all the attention he was getting from his novel. She also referenced that he was very insecure about his Jewishness and viewed it as a problem.

When Miller was eighteen, the two had sex and the very next day Salinger sent her home on a plane. That was it. Miller remembers maybe getting one or two more letters after that. He sent her home under the pretense that she had come between him and his work. He was the first man with whom she had sex. The more plausible reason is that once they had sex she no longer represented the youthfulness or innocence that he may have compulsively sought in young women. At play here is a tragic paradox that plagued Salinger for the rest of his life and played a huge role in his decision to quit publishing after 1965 and reject the public: the very young women that he sought for their youth and innocence essentially were stripped of these very qualities by him. Subsequently, along with the relationships being exploitative and criminal, they had zero chance of lasting.[18]

Arguably, Salinger's interest in young women was set in motion when he was brutally jilted by his first love Oona O'Neill, daughter of playwright Eugene O'Neill, whom Salinger first met in the summer of 1941 before he joined the army. Eugene O'Neill had won the Nobel Prize five years earlier and certainly Salinger was enamored with the fact that he was dating the man's daughter. Likewise, Oona was impressed that Salinger was an up-and-coming writer who had already placed a few stories in magazines like *Esquire* and *Collier's*. Oona had a rocky relationship with her alcoholic father, who had walked out on the family with another woman when Oona was a little girl. At the time Salinger was twenty-two and Oona was sixteen. Nevertheless, that summer Salinger fell deeply in love with her and the two enjoyed New York City together. While Salinger was dating Oona right before the war, he was working on *The Catcher in the Rye*. Meanwhile, Oona was being photographed at the Stork Club hanging out with the rich and famous and appearing in the papers the following day. One year later Salinger joined the army and entered the war, and Oona left for Hollywood and married Charlie Chaplin. Oona simply quit responding to Salinger's letters even though he thought the two were still an item. He read about Oona's marriage in the paper like everyone else. This experience for Salinger likely set in motion a lifetime of trying to recapture what he felt he had with Oona. She not only represented a beautiful woman on the brink of the rest of her life, but she also represented life before the war, when Salinger was on the cusp of making it as a writer and marrying into a famed literary family. She was sixteen when they were dating, the same age as Holden in *The Catcher in the Rye*. A girl having an alcoholic father would also be the case in other young girls' lives whom he seduced. That his experiences right after this devastating relationship were war experiences may have calcified his ideas and memories regarding Oona and the illusive future in front of them, causing these illusions to grow distorted in their meaning and beauty and innocence.

Holden's account of all the crazy stuff that happened the Christmas prior to him going to California that he relates to his psychoanalyst begins the day he leaves Pencey Prep, game day Saturday, a day notorious in America for sexual violence against women. Although *The Catcher in the Rye* takes place in the late 1940s, recent studies have linked sports with sexual violence, suggesting a correlation that likely stretches back to the time in which the novel takes place. According to Maxwell Strachan, "Rapes rise by 41 percent on the day of home football games at FBS schools. Reports of college-aged offenders raping college-aged victims rise by 58 percent on the day of home football games. . . . Football games appear to lead to as many as 770 rapes at FBS schools every year."[19] These statistics underscore a troubling link between male sports culture and sexual violence that informs much of the action of *The Catcher in the Rye*. The book highlights the link between sports and systemic sexual violence by characterizing Holden's roommate Stradlater, a basketball star at Pencey, as an athlete who seduces young girls in a car illegally provided by the coach.

Holden finds out on Saturday night that Stradlater, whom he describes as hypersexual, plans to take out Jane Gallagher, a former friend of Holden's who he thinks may have been molested by her stepfather. Holden describes Stradlater as a guy whose boasts about women are actually true. This single event preoccupies Holden throughout the rest of the novel and fuels his contempt for the exaggerated male behavior prevalent at Pencey Prep, especially among athletes. Holden relates how the Pencey Prep basketball coach Ed Banky secretly allows some of his players, including Stradlater, to borrow his car to take out girls. Holden characterizes himself as a weak guy compared to Stradlater, who he says is very strong and handsome. Further, he details how Stradlater ignores girls when they refuse his sexual advances even when they very clearly tell him to stop. Notably, Holden also takes advantage of Stradlater's car privileges by double-dating and using the car as a potential space in which to seduce women. These contradictions in Holden represent a pattern whereby Holden, like his author, criticizes male behavior that he also at times enacts.

Holden's particular emotional reaction to the prospect of Stradlater taking out Jane stems in part from Holden's suspicion that Jane has already been a victim of sexual violence at the hands of her stepfather. Holden's knowledge of Jane's childhood and relationship with her stepfather triggers his penchant for protecting the vulnerable.

The idea that Stradlater may have preyed upon a vulnerable girl whom Holden cares about and who may have already been sexually abused is too much for Holden to handle. When Stradlater returns from the date late Saturday night, Holden confronts him. Stradlater has no idea why Holden is so upset and dispatches him quickly but not before Holden seethes with accusation. This early scene in the book establishes Holden's limited willingness to defend the vulnerable, including women, and his hostility toward exaggerated male behavior, as well as his penchant for performing the very behavior that he criticizes. His response to Stradlater's sexual aggression is to be violently aggressive himself.

Michael Kimmel defines the brand of male behavior that Holden is critical of as "marketplace masculinity," marked mostly by aggressiveness and competition. Notably, aggression and competition evoke athletics, especially football. Kimmel further points out that "violence is often the single most evident marker of manhood"[20] and that over time masculinity has been defined as the rejection of the feminine.[21] While Stradlater initially embodies marketplace masculinity insofar as he is an athlete and notorious womanizer, Holden first displays the marketplace masculinity marker of violence. As far as Stradlater is concerned, he is only demonstrating his constant sexual availability, a staple in traditional American masculinity. Holden's violent response indicates both his willingness to defend Jane and his investment in the very behavior he vilifies. He grapples with this paradox throughout the novel.

Along with various small acts of violence and fantasies about violence, several times throughout the novel Holden discusses sexual aggressiveness and violence, reinforcing the correlation between exaggerated maleness and violence, including sexual violence. Various forms of subtle and not so subtle sexual aggressiveness occur throughout the novel to both women and men.

In addition to Holden's characterization of Stradlater as a potential rapist, Holden witnesses other instances of sexual aggression. He notices these aggressions largely because of his preoccupation with Jane, whom he constantly brings up. What he points out is colored through the lens of his concern for her.

When he visits his sister Phoebe's school, he finds that someone has defaced the property by scrawling obscenities on the wall. His violent reaction is similar to his reaction to the prospect of Stradlater raping Jane. For Holden, the world is sullied by sexual aggressors who ruin everything. Part of being the catcher in the rye is protecting victims from sexual violence in the hopes of providing a safe space. Holden's penchant for violence as a legitimate response to sexual aggressiveness marks his closeted indictment of macho maleness. Throughout much of the novel Holden struggles to demonstrate an alternative version of masculinity to accompany his criticisms of it.

For Holden, phony macho performance drives rape culture. His hostility toward this sort of inauthenticity accounts in part for his criticism of movies and especially actors. The exaggerated male behavior that Holden vilifies is based in large part on a gender performance that in many cases leads to sexual violence. In other words, men perform their manliness in order to live up to a macho standard that often leads to aggression and violence. The notion that only women perform gender because of the obvious accoutrements of feminine performance such as long hair, dresses, and makeup further complicates macho performance that contradistinctively appears fixed and unchanging. The myth of innate or fixed maleness represents a dangerous idea since it suggests that men have no option other than to deal with it as an immutable standard that they either live up to or fail to meet. While Holden rightly views macho behavior as a destructively performed social construction, he often fails to enact an alternative.

For Holden, the locus of exaggerated male performance starts with Pencey Prep and its marketing strategy. The staged nature of Pencey Prep is also reflected in the men who represent Pencey. Holden's general indictment of phoniness centers on the macho performance of the leaders at Pencey. To him, the phoniness of the male culture drives male behavior and the desire for the symbols of male success, that is, cars and women.

Holden's distaste for phony macho performance also drives his ambivalent feelings about movies, and especially male actors, whom he views as embodiments of macho behavior. The reason why he hates actors is the same reason he hates most of the men at Pencey. In both cases, male authenticity is undermined by a desire to *appear* macho. Holden feels that men and actors represent male macho stereotypes. Holden applies the criteria by which he attacks male actors to nonactors as well, such as the man to whom he is introduced by one of D.B.'s old girlfriends who appears to want to break his hand when he shakes it.

In addition to Holden criticizing phony male culture and worrying about Jane Gallagher, he often makes excuses or otherwise apologizes for his lack of sexual success, evincing the closeted status of his position. He confesses his virginity as though it reflects a flaw in his makeup. Even though he is clearly critical of Stradlater's sexual aggressiveness, he fails to fully disavow the idea that a man ought to always be on the make and sexually available when it comes to women.

Holden's inability to confidently condemn sexual aggressiveness reflects his closeted criticism of hyperbolic male behavior. He is clearly still invested in traditional male socialization, and the book can be read as his slowly building confidence in his feelings of compassion toward women and other marginalized groups, alternative masculinities, perversions, and sexualities.

When Maurice asks Holden whether he is interested in a girl that night, Maurice assesses Holden's manhood. Holden realizes later that the lowlife pimp Maurice is also a phony, symbolized by the fact that all he wears underneath his elevator operator's uniform is a collar with no shirt. The prostitute Sunny then becomes a kind of currency between the two men. Maurice assesses Holden's manhood as below par only because Holden allows him to do so. While Holden's actions once he is alone with Sunny indicate that his principles will not allow him to totally objectify and sexually exploit her as well as his attempt to view her as a human being rather than a sexual commodity, the fact that he has agreed to the trade already dooms him. He has allowed himself to engage with the pimp Maurice, and therefore his manhood is at stake. Once Holden is alone with Sunny, she regards him suspiciously since he is not performing his male role appropriately. Holden's failure to perform with Sunny even when he does not want to humiliates him. Sunny's expectations are for Holden to exploit her sexually rather than treat her like a human being. On top of this, and as a result of Holden's failure to enact an alternative way of being a man, Sunny and Maurice return and demand more money from Holden. Eventually, the two of them take an additional five dollars out of his wallet, double what they quoted him, and shamefully Holden begins to cry. Maurice then snaps his finger on Holden's genitals as a symbol of Holden's and perhaps the author's phallic lack. Holden's lackluster attempt to compete in this male arena not only prevents him from possibly acting as a change agent or catcher in the rye for Sunny, who seems to be fairly new to the profession, but it also results in humiliation and violence.

This scene marks the second time Holden gets beaten up, and both times they symbolize his failure within an arena of which Holden is critical. Further, both times Holden folds the experience into a fantasy wherein his failure actually symbolizes his maleness. His response to his beatdowns by both Stradlater and Maurice is a male fantasy wherein he is a gangster hero. His penchant for recouping his manhood within the confines of exaggerated maleness through fantasy points to the closet in which his overall indictment lies. After he is humiliated and robbed by Sunny and Maurice, Holden enacts a full-fledged fantasy drama straight out of a Humphrey Bogart film.

Holden's fantasy reward for his heroism would be Jane herself since Holden's real failure and the one he is most preoccupied with is not protecting Jane from Stradlater, not being her catcher in the rye.

Holden's choice of Bogart as a role model is significant insofar as Bogart represents the very pinnacle of urbane suave manhood, again suggesting Holden's closeted and ambivalent hostility toward macho maleness.

Holden's fantasies about being wounded both recoup his manhood and play into the symbolism of being morally flawed. Throughout the text, Holden lies about being terminally ill or on the brink of death. His penchant for telling people that he has a severe physical problem symbolizes his phallic lack and his feeling that his inability to fully embrace exaggerated maleness represents a severe flaw in his gender makeup.

After Holden leaves Pencey, still bloody from Stradlater's beatdown, he tells the mother of a Pencey student that he has a tumor. Likewise, he tells Sunny that he cannot sleep with her because he has a physical defect.

Another telling response to Holden's emasculation at the hands of Maurice and Sunny is his admission that he felt like committing suicide. This admission links him with James Castle, the boy who was assaulted by other Pencey Prep students and who commits suicide by jumping out of his dorm window. Castle is not a part of the male culture at Pencey because of his weakness compared to the other boys, just like Holden describes himself in relation to Stradlater. As Maurice likely snaps Holden on his privates, very likely the boys who assaulted Castle did something similar and likely worse. Castle then may have jumped out of the window because the boys essentially humiliated him by raping or sexually assaulting him. Further, Holden identifies with Castle since Castle died wearing Holden's sweater. By contrast, Holden loans Stradlater his houndstooth jacket the night Stradlater takes out Jane, symbolizing Holden's identification with both Castle and Stradlater and his ambivalence with regard to aggressive male culture. Whatever actually did occur between Stradlater and Jane the night Holden left Pencey, Stradlater was wearing Holden's jacket.

Mr. Antolini attempts to be Holden's spiritual advisor and possibly his potential guide into the realm of alternative sexualities. He recognizes and comments on Holden's distaste for macho maleness. Despite Holden railing against athletes to the reader and to his analyst, he is not ready to admit this to Antolini since he is essentially in the closet about his distaste for macho masculinity. Consequently, Holden responds by denying Antolini's charge, especially in relation to Stradlater. Here again Holden, by way of association, admits to the reader that he associates Stradlater with athletes and men whom Holden cannot stand, particularly those who perform exaggerated versions of maleness that Holden cannot seem to master but fails to fully disavow when the chips are down. One can easily draw a parallel here between Holden and Stradlater and Salinger and Hemingway. Antolini brushes off Holden's denial and encourages him to seek out other male writers who share Holden's worldview and inability to mesh with macho men. Antolini then asks Holden about his women right after this, hinting that he suspects Holden might be homosexual or at the very least confused about his sexuality, something that Holden admits throughout the novel.

Holden's description of Antolini and his wife suggests that they do not have much of a romantic relationship and merely perform the roles of husband and wife in order to appear as such to the outside world to protect Antolini.

The next indication of Antolini's sexuality is Antolini's inappropriate behavior toward Holden. Holden shares with his analyst and the reader that this was not the first time that someone has made a pass at him, possibly an older man. The importance of this scene centers on Holden's intense homophobic reaction to Antolini—likely an indication of his own sexual insecurity—as well as his eventual reluctance to dismiss Antolini as a sexual predator or deviant. Ultimately Holden cannot morally condemn Antolini for his homosexuality since Holden is unsure of himself in that arena and is sympathetic to the marginalized. In light of Salinger's own predilection for very young romantic partners, the compassion with which Holden ultimately treats Antolini is telling and may betray Salinger's sympathy for such a dynamic.

Antolini fails to actually help Holden, not because of Antolini's probable homosexuality, but more likely because the man is drunk. Antolini represents simply one of several older men who fail to advise Holden in any meaningful way. Another older man who fails to advise Holden and who also happens to be very likely gay is Carl Luce, an upperclassman at Whooton whom Holden lauds as being very smart but likely a homosexual. After Holden calls him up, Luce suggests that they have a drink in a bar Holden describes as a bar frequented by homosexuals, whom he calls flits.

Like Antolini, Luce is older and was at one time supposed to be an advisor to Holden. Instead of advising the students with regard to their studies, Luce appears to have advised them in the arena of nonnormative sexualities. What strikes Holden as particularly interesting is the folks whom Luce suggest are in the closet, specifically very masculine men. Holden spends half the novel attacking exaggerated male performance and phony tough guys and half the novel aping their behavior while staying in the closet as to his distaste for it. The idea that exaggerated male performance could actually point to homosexuality both excites Holden because it points to the phoniness of men but also scares him regarding his own sexuality. While he is clearly sympathetic to alternative sexualities, he is unsure how to voice those sympathies without compromising his own sense of himself as a heterosexual man. Like Antolini, Holden considers Luce a possible homosexual but also an intelligent man, the mark of his version of an ideal man embodied in his dead brother Allie.

Holden's desire for a meaningful sexual experience frustrates him. His respect for women doubles as a perceived flaw in himself and accounts for his feeling that something is morally wrong with him. Luce, who is very likely gay and, like Antolini, in the closet, reads Holden's admission as evidence of his latent homosexuality and suggests conversion therapy. The subtext of this conversation suggests that Luce has struggled with his own sexuality and with the help of his psychoanalyst father has remained in the closet. Luce's subtle suggestion that Holden see a psychoanalyst for his sexual deviance functions as an ironic criticism of Holden's entire confession presented to the reader as the text of the novel. In this light, the novel symbolizes the beginning of Holden's conversion therapy.

Holden interacts with two men in the closet, Antolini and Luce, and therefore receives very little instruction in how best to function as a man unsatisfied with macho male culture. What keeps Antolini and Luce in the closet and what keeps Holden in the closet in terms of his sympathy for diverse sexualities is the belief that real men must maintain a level of masculinity that reflects a repudiation of the feminine. Holden struggles between overcoming his desire to be manly and his sympathy for anyone who is oppressed and his role as the catcher in the rye of the persecuted. Further, Holden's closeted antimacho stance causes him to wonder whether something is wrong with him, whether he has a problem with his hormones. He continually cites his respect for women as a flaw. Holden cannot seem to reject macho masculinity or accept alternative sexualities without fearing effeminacy or a sort of literal transformation symbolized by a sickness within.

An early version of the character Carl Luce and the scene in which he and Holden meet for a drink appear in the story "Slight Rebellion off Madison." In the early version, there is no mention of Luce being gay or the bar in which they meet being a gay bar or flitty. That was all clearly added in later drafts, suggesting that Salinger purposefully altered Luce from a fat and unattractive boy to a vaguely gay intellectual.

Despite Holden's fear of becoming feminized due to his distaste for exaggerated male behavior, in other works through other characters, namely, Buddy Glass, a writer fashioned after Salinger himself, Salinger has voiced the value of androgyny in a writer and the narrow-mindedness of dwelling too much on sex and gender. In *Raise High the Roof Beam, Carpenters and Seymour: An Introduction*, Buddy Glass relates a story that his older brother Seymour read to their younger sister Franny when she was young. The story centers on a seer who has the ability to assess the value of horses even though he often mistakes their breed and sex. Later in the novel, Buddy Glass further notes that great writers are able to embody androgyny through their characters. These two passages point to Salinger's interest in gender constructs if not realization of the destructiveness of fearing femininity.

Throughout *The Catcher in the Rye*, Holden displays an unusual understanding and sympathy for perversions that may stem from Salinger's self-professed deformity and his sexual proclivities. Once Holden gets to his hotel in New York, he notices several strange occurrences through the window in the other rooms, including a cross-dresser. Holden's reaction to the man is decidedly low key. Holden then makes a light comparison to himself, implying that he is really no better.

One can argue that Salinger's physical deformity and his sexual preference for young girls made him sympathetic with diverse sexualities, and what complicates Holden's sense of himself in the novel revolves around his confusion regarding his sympathy for these same diverse sexualities and the implication that he has had same-sex sexual experiences. For Holden, and perhaps for Salinger, diverse sexualities equate perversions, but their own sexual diversity prevents them from vilifying these perversions.

Holden's equanimity vis-à-vis sexual perversions casts his desire to be the catcher in the rye in a whole new light. Along with being the catcher in the rye for the oppressed, he also wants to be the catcher in the rye for the sexually diverse. The irony here is that while Holden wants to be a catcher in the rye for children, he is also interested in protecting the marginalized and perverted from persecution and the hostility of macho culture. Holden would then be charged with protecting the author as well as the young girls the author preyed upon his whole life. So perhaps Salinger created a character who could both protect children and himself and children from himself.

If the marker of macho behavior is violence, then Holden's brother Allie is the antithesis of this. Further, if what drives Holden through much of the novel is his preoccupation with Stradlater and Jane and whether Stradlater was overaggressive with Jane in Coach Banky's car, Allie emerges as a sort of antidote to Stradlater and the kind of jock rape culture Holden rails against. For example, Stradlater is a member of the basketball team and is granted special privileges because of it, namely, access to Banky's car in which Holden believes Stradlater often gets aggressive with girls. The number one physical symbol of Allie and the subject of the essay that Holden writes for Stradlater is Allie's baseball glove, a sports artifact that Allie has transformed into a vehicle for poetry. Holden thinks so much of the baseball mitt that he actually has it with him at Pencey. Also, in contrast to many of the men Holden rails against for being stupid, Holden notes that Allie was very smart and that his death was extremely hard on Holden. Illustrating the importance of Allie as a figure in the novel, when Phoebe asks Holden to name one thing he likes, he cites his dead brother.

For Holden, the existence of his brother despite the fact that he died suggests a positive example for Holden and a way to avoid the fate Antolini forecasts for him, that he is preparing for a great fall into a hole that will never allow him to hit bottom driven by his distaste for humanity, especially other men. The existence of Allie as a model for a type of man that is in direct conflict with macho masculinity bodes well for Holden's eventual recovery. Allie represents a sort of savior for Holden, a version of maleness that Holden can embrace that has the power to transform a baseball mitt into a vehicle for poetry. In death, Allie is able to accomplish what the other men in the novel fail to do: provide Holden with instruction about how to be a man in the world without exploiting it or other people in the process. If we equate Salinger with Holden, then Salinger's ideal human being is eleven years old and nonexistent or, at least, dead and so therefore incorruptible by time.

In *The Catcher in the Rye*, despite Holden opening up to his psychoanalyst and indirectly to the reader, he is in the closet about a whole host of aspects about himself. For example, Holden is in the closet about his Jewishness; Holden is in the closet about his sympathies for what he views as perversions; Holden is also in the closet potentially about his own sexuality or at least the fear that he might be a homosexual, driven perhaps by different experiences with other boys or much older men. Further, Holden is in the closet about his distaste for macho masculinity and his inability to live up to these definitions. On one hand, it bodes well that Holden is unburdening himself to his psychoanalyst, but on the other, sharing all this does not necessarily mean he will be able to escape his depression.

Simply because we witness Holden unburdening himself to his psychoanalyst does not mean that the psychoanalyst will help Holden. The fear is that the psychoanalyst will solidify Holden's belief that there is something wrong with him, that his sympathy toward perversions is something that needs to be eradicated. Consequently, rather than trying to normalize a new version of maleness represented by his dead brother, Allie, the psychoanalyst may diagnose Holden himself as a pervert. In *Franny and Zooey*, Salinger depicts therapy as destructive and it seems clear that Salinger wants zero part of anyone being diagnosed as a pervert, most of all himself.

Holden's character is an echo of the modernist tradition of presenting a protagonist with two choices, either to conform to cultural standards or to disintegrate into neuroses. Holden's neuroses function as a protest of the evils of society, including masculinity, and this becomes the human condition under late capitalism. One either goes with the flow, or goes crazy.[22] Salinger then walks in the footsteps of Joyce, Beckett, Faulkner, and Kafka by presenting a character who reflects a diseased culture but does not have the capacity to effect change within that culture. Considering the massive response to the novel and decades of readers identifying with Holden, this dynamic indicates a cultural attitude of apathy and renunciation in relation to a broken society too immense to change.

Holden's primary preoccupations in *The Catcher in the Rye* have to do with Jane Gallagher and Allie. Holden struggles with his inability to save Jane from the likes of her stepfather and Stradlater, who represent a rape culture fueled by macho maleness to which he views Allie as an alternative, despite his crystallized eleven years of age. Holden's inability to be the catcher in the rye for Jane stems from his inability to fully disavow a masculine culture that he views as inherently phony and fake. His reluctance to come out against this culture renders him closeted about a whole host of feelings and views, including his sympathy with nonnormative sexualities and perversions possibly informed by Salinger's insecurities regarding his testicular deformity and romantic and sexual feelings toward very young girls. Despite some critics viewing the ending of the book as positive in that Holden confesses his feelings, his therapeutic confession does not actually bode well for his future and possibly suggests his diagnosis as a mentally unstable pervert, a diagnosis Salinger himself likely feared throughout his life.

The idea that the events in a novel and the psyche of the protagonist within that novel depend in large part if not entirely on the author is not a profound idea in and of itself. Novels are creations and reflections of their author as well as the culture in which the author lives. *The Catcher in the Rye* is no exception. The birth of the novel and the events within it as well as Holden Caulfield can be explained in large part by Salinger's experiences in World War II as a Jew. Race cannot be ignored in the novel, but like whiteness in relation to white people, it has for the most part been missed or minimized. Likewise, Salinger's sense of himself as a man and his relationships with young women also cannot be ignored. This aspect of the author drove the story of the novel after it was published. The novel's life after publication has as much to do with the author's eventual refusal to publish and his decision to shun his readers as the novel itself, and this decision on the part of the author was about his fear of being labeled a pervert.

2

CATCHER IN THE FIFTIES

Sweet Sixteen and the King

When the 1950s began, there was reason for optimism. Hitler and the Nazis had been defeated and anti-Semitism was no longer in vogue, causing some to naively hope that other forms of racial, sexual, and religious hate were also on the way out. The United States enjoyed an economic boom and witnessed a wildly transforming culture, especially in music, fashion, and art. In retrospect, there was good reason for optimism, but with twenty-twenty hindsight there was also good reason for sobering pessimism, as the civil rights movement, Vietnam War, and Cold War were just getting under way. The decade of the 1950s was an opportunity for all Americans to come out of the closet as a people of inclusion, the antithesis to the Nazi hate machine that analogized a group of people to a virus plaguing the state and then vowed to eradicate that virus through systematic murder. Both J. D. Salinger and Elvis Presley emerged in the decade as artists with the potential to culturally lead the way through literature and music toward building a country that stood for the opposite of what the Nazis stood for. Salinger and Elvis had a chance to demonstrate that diversity could be a form of healing, and as Hemingway noted, that the healing could make the broken places even stronger. Salinger's greatest contribution to this worthy endeavor was *The Catcher in the Rye*, an antiestablishment, antiwhite supremacy novel that augured the arrival of a serious artist unafraid to take on the more insidious aspects of American exceptionalism still haunting the American cultural landscape.

Elvis's contribution was a new form of wildly popular music that melded white southern culture with African American culture. Unfortunately, by the end of the decade neither artist would make good on his promise beyond his initial foray and the 1950s would instead be known as a decade of conformity.

Before *The Catcher in the Rye* was even published, Salinger was already scampering back into his closet. In 1949, not long after his short story "Uncle Wiggily in Connecticut" appeared in the *New Yorker*, Samuel Goldwyn purchased the film rights to it from Salinger. In exchange for the handsome payday, Salinger gave up all creative rights. This was the first time Salinger had sold any of his work to Hollywood and would be the primary reason why *The Catcher in the Rye* was never made into a film.[1]

In the short story, two former college roommates, Eloise and Mary Jane, meet up at Eloise's home not long after World War II in an upper-middle-class Connecticut suburb during a snowstorm. The two drink heavily and the afternoon unravels into a drunken morass wherein Eloise expresses her dissatisfaction with her husband, Lew, and her deep sadness concerning the love of her life Walt who died in the war in an absurd accident where a Japanese stove blew up while Lew and a few other men were trying to wrap it up and send it home for their colonel. The emotional locus of the story centers on Eloise's daughter Ramona who overhears the two women discussing Walt and her father, Lew, and bitterly and reactively announces that her imaginary friend Jimmy Jimmereeno has been run over by a car. At the end of the story, Eloise checks on her daughter only to find her sleeping on one side of the bed in order to make room for her new replacement imaginary friend Mickey Mickeranno. Eloise intuits the parallel behavior of replacing nonexistent men with other nearly nonexistent men and reacts angrily. In addition to the main plot of the story, a subplot revolves around the way Eloise treats her black maid Grace. At times Eloise describes Grace as foolish and lazy and complains that instead of fetching the two women their drinks that Grace is likely sitting on her butt. Eloise also mentions that she ran into one of the girls' college friends who told her that in Europe she had nearly been raped by a black soldier. These exchanges set up a revealing moment several pages later where Grace asks Eloise whether or not her husband can stay the night instead of going home in a blizzard and risking his life and limb. Eloise, of course, says no and that she is not running a hotel, the implication being that the black husband cannot be trusted to not rape the white women in the house.

When Salinger watched the film version of his short story in 1950 called *My Foolish Heart*, he was horrified. The same screenwriters who had written *Casablanca*, Julius and Philip Epstein, butchered Salinger's short story into a procrustean tearjerker love story centered on Eloise and Lew. The film team denuded nearly everything in the story that was important to Salinger, and close to all of Salinger's pet themes were on full display. As with *The Catcher in the Rye*, the story indicts affluent whiteness and exposes its exclusionary hierarchical and racist construction. Grace and her husband are characterized by the WASPy Eloise as lazy, unintelligent, and hypersexual while Eloise and Mary Jane fritter the day away drinking and whining about their charmed lives. Additionally, Salinger once again employs a prominent child character and imposes on that child a budding sexuality in the form of her imaginary male friends with whom she sleeps. Further, Salinger alludes to the absurdity of war in the form of Walt's tragic but ridiculous death by way of an exploding stove. Indictments of war, whiteness, and racism and the use of a sexualized child mark this tale as one of Salinger's most signature stories. Most, if not all, of these themes are absent or very much muted in the film. The film ends with Eloise promising to be a good girl and good wife to Lew whereas the story ends with a drunken Eloise desperately asking a drunken Mary Jane whether she is a good girl. As a result of this experience, Salinger never again sold any of his work to Hollywood despite being offered millions of dollars from the likes of Elia Kazan, Billy Wilder, Steven Spielberg, and Harvey Weinstein.

Notwithstanding the scathing reviews that accused the film of being emotionally manipulative and terribly sentimental, the movie went on to win multiple Academy Awards and the song "My Foolish Heart" from the film became an American classic. Salinger certainly felt humiliated that forever his short story—which was such a harsh indictment of upper-class whiteness—would be associated with a cultural product that reinforced the very thing he had attacked. What further must have incensed Salinger was the knowledge that he had sold out, taken money for his work, and in the process stripped it of its power. He himself had become implicit in the very culture he derided. Having his bitingly pessimistic short story turned into a cheesy romantic comedy no doubt played a role in Holden Caulfield's hatred of films and Hollywood in the novel that would come out a few years later.

One can understand Salinger's initial desire to have the story turned into a film. Many of his literary heroes, such as Fitzgerald and Hemingway, had made forays into the Hollywood machine. Like publishing in the *New Yorker*, Salinger felt as though selling a story to Hollywood represented a benchmark in his career. What differentiated Salinger from these other writers was the intensity with which Salinger dealt with certain themes and the guardedness and secrecy and crippling insecurity that came along with it. "Uncle Wiggily in Connecticut" harbors all of Salinger's skeletons: his penchant for young girls, his war wounds, his hatred of the white power structure, and his sympathy for the marginalized. For him, it must have felt courageous to offer his work to the world, sublime even in the risk that he must have felt that he was taking, only to realize that the risk was not the kind of risk he thought it was at all but something different. Maybe it was this experience that eventually drove him to not publish at all, the realization that once he released his work to the masses it was no longer his but its own thing with a biography and a life all its own driven by a public and readership with the power to impose meaning and even change up the plot though the words remained the same on the page.

In 1951, sixteen-year-old junior high schooler Elvis Presley, the same age as the protagonist Holden Caulfield in the novel *The Catcher in the Rye* published two months prior, tried out for the football team. His decision to play football was odd for a number of reasons. First of all, 1951 was the year Elvis first grew out his sideburns and began using more Vaseline on his hair.[2] This was the year that he generally began fashioning an image different from the other boys in his class who looked like replicas of their fathers. By his senior year, he would be wearing slacks to school every day instead of jeans like the other boys, along with pink shirts and scarves and pants with a stripe down the side. Two years prior, his family had moved to Memphis from East Tupelo where they had lived in an upscale black neighborhood. In Tupelo, Elvis brought his guitar to school and would play for his classmates with only the slightest encouragement.

By contrast, he was cripplingly shy his first year in Memphis, but in his junior year he began to come out of his closet little by little, surrendering to the impulse that compelled him to set himself apart from the other boys in his class and in his neighborhood. For a sensitive young man in the first delicate stages of developing his individualism, mostly marked by his passion for music, joining the football team seemed ill advised.

Elvis had already experienced bullying from other, rougher boys. Once in Tupelo, a few of his male classmates held him down, stole his guitar, and cut the strings.[3] Perhaps one of the reasons that he was bullied was because he so obviously preferred the company of women. He clearly felt more comfortable around women, and was especially close to his mother. He often played his guitar and sang when there were just girls around but clammed up around other boys or men.[4] For a boy who preferred the company of women and who had already been bullied in the past by other boys, the gridiron was a treacherous space.

Predictably, football was a disaster. While he made the team, he did not last long, ostensibly because he refused to cut his hair. One day after practice, a group of players ganged up on him and threatened to cut it. Perhaps they caught him just as he was changing out of his pads. Maybe he was half-naked. Maybe they pinned him down and called him names. If it was not for Red West, who would go on to be an All-Memphis football player and a lifelong friend of Elvis's, coming to his aid before things got really ugly, there was a chance these other boys would have humiliated Elvis even worse than James Castle was humiliated in *The Catcher in the Rye*. As a result of the incident, Elvis got kicked off the team. The other boys went unpunished.[5]

Elvis's refusal to conform to jock standards in high school represents only one instance of the King refusing to conform to macho white male culture when he was a young man in the 1950s. Two years later in 1953, Elvis recorded his first record in Sun Studios in Memphis, a studio created by Sam Phillips expressly to accommodate black singers who at the time had no place open to them in which to record their music.[6] Despite the many other hungry young singers and musicians eager to make the big time, Elvis was one of the few who actually came by the studio looking to cut a record. The King showed up armed with a child's guitar, a quavering voice, and a host of slave songs that he knew by heart. Perhaps the others were turned off by the studio's overtly catering to African American musicians. Not Elvis. Elvis grew up around black people and black culture and had no qualms about the possibility of recording in a black space. In early recording sessions, Elvis certainly recorded songs based on black spirituals and gospel music developed on antebellum slave plantations by slaves who used the songs to communicate and plan escapes under the noses of their slave masters.

Nevertheless, in Jim Crow Tennessee in the 1950s, even for Elvis there were limits. The degree to which Elvis was willing to come out of the closet as a man who did not care about race is best illustrated by his clandestine excursions to black churches with his girlfriend, aptly named Dixie, to hear the black church music that blew them both away. His regular church, First Assembly, featured a fire-and-brimstone preacher by the name of Pastor James Hamill and a congregation that would at times speak in tongues. Sometimes Elvis and Dixie would sneak out of First Assembly and drive over to the exotic black church where the music was far better. Elvis and Dixie would only stay a few minutes because they were fearful of being missed by Reverend Hamill, but for those few minutes Elvis and Dixie were out of the closet. [7]

There is little doubt that Elvis was thoroughly influenced by black culture and that not hiding that influence was a risk on his part. Elvis's look and sound stemmed from the blues clubs on Beale Street and radio stations that primarily featured black artists. Early in his career, he admitted that musicians of color had been playing the way he played and moving the way he moved long before he started doing it. In addition to the music, his hairstyle and the outfits he wore were inspired by black cultural styles often purchased at black stores in the area. In those early days, he enjoyed a crossover appeal and seemed to be interested in creating a new form of music rather than merely imitating an existing one. [8] Elvis's obvious black cultural influences even caused many established and famous country music singers to refer to Elvis as a white nigger.

Like Salinger's sixteen-year-old protagonist in *The Catcher in the Rye* Holden Caulfield, Elvis's struggles when he was sixteen were in relation to masculinity and race. Like Holden, Elvis clearly felt ambivalent about male culture in the 1950s and struggled to navigate his way through it in relation to developing a sense of himself as an individual and a man. Elvis also clearly had to navigate the minefield of race as a man who grew up around African Americans and did not hesitate to record in a studio meant for black musicians or to visit a black church just as Holden has to deal with his Jewishness in a time when it was vilified.

It had been a decade since Salinger's heartbreaking split with Oona O'Neil, five years since his failed marriage to a Nazi informant, and just two years since his dalliance with fourteen-year-old Jean Miller, when in

1951 Salinger attended a party hosted by Francis Steegmuller, a writer from the *New Yorker*, and his wife Bee Stein. There he met sixteen-year-old Claire Douglas, the daughter of a famous British art dealer. The following day Salinger contacted the Steegmullers and was given Claire's address at Shipley, the same private school Jane Gallagher attends in *The Catcher in the Rye*. The two began dating immediately.[9] Shortly thereafter Salinger began referring to a girl that he was thinking about marrying named Mary. Very likely Mary was Claire. Salinger's secrecy and apparent shame in dating such a young girl was apparently there from the start. The two were still dating in 1953 when Claire was nineteen and attending Radcliffe. Salinger wanted Claire to quit school and join him in Cornish, New Hampshire, where he had moved that year, a pattern that would continue for the rest of his life. Claire refused to quit school and join Salinger in rural New Hampshire and instead began dating a Harvard Business School MBA student named Colman M. Mockler. The two even spent the summer together in Europe, which infuriated Salinger. The next year Claire and Mockler were married, but a few months later Claire left Mockler for the author who was her sixteen-year senior and had the marriage annulled. In 1955, Salinger and Claire were married in Cornish, and in December the two had a child named Margaret Ann.[10]

Salinger's relationship with Claire Douglas proved many things. First off, Claire exemplified the degree to which Salinger based his characters on real-life human beings, as she was very likely the basis for Jane Gallagher from *Catcher*, Franny from *Franny and Zooey*, and possibly Esmé in "For Esmé—with Love and Squalor"; though some would argue Esmé was based more on Jean Miller because Esmé is English, Claire is more likely the model for the character. His relationship with Claire also instantiated his penchant for very young women and the concomitant guilt, shame, and secrecy that inevitably followed. It is interesting to note that the two began dating in 1951 when Claire was sixteen, the same age as Holden and the same age as Elvis Presley the year the novel was published, as well as the same age as Oona when Salinger began dating her. That Salinger kept Claire a secret and referred to her in letters as Mary points to the never-ending closet in which he lived and suffered and possibly another reason why he eventually quit publishing and rejected the public that adored him.

Elvis and Salinger are an interesting pair to consider side by side. Salinger's sexual desire for very young girls reminds one of all the young girls who surely swooned over the King at his concerts. If Claire represents Jane, and in *The Catcher in the Rye* it is hinted that Jane was molested by her stepfather, and Holden is a stand-in for Salinger and wishes to be the catcher in the rye for Jane, who does the real-life Salinger actually represent, Holden, or the stepfather, or both?

By all accounts, Claire's life in Cornish was difficult. Salinger swallowed up anything he touched and absconded with it into his closet, Claire included. The two had a second child in 1960, and in 1966 Claire filed for divorce, citing that Salinger had emotionally abandoned her and that her health had taken a drastic turn for the worse. Claire got everything in the settlement except a nearby plot of land that Salinger had recently purchased and on which he built another house.

In 1951, shortly after the publication of *The Catcher in the Rye* and before he moved to Cornish, New Hampshire, and around the time that he was courting or otherwise involved with the sixteen-year-old Claire Douglas, Salinger retreated from his budding fame into a monastic-like apartment in Manhattan at 300 East Fifty-Seventh Street. The apartment was sparsely decorated with black furniture. The only thing on the wall was a portrait of the artist in uniform.[11] We might think of his apartment as a sort of self-imposed closet where Salinger could hide from the world while his book and Holden Caulfield did all the talking. His self-imposed closet that held not only his sexual proclivities but also his religion became a space in which he attempted to confront both of these items in his life. This is around the time Salinger became involved in Vedanta, a form of Eastern Hindu philosophy that stressed sexual restraint. It is hard not to think that Salinger's attraction to Vedanta in part was driven by his overwhelming interest in very young girls. Vedanta teaches that there is only one God and that God is present in all things. The goal for a believer is to achieve God-consciousness through uninterrupted contemplation of a deity. From this point forward, the Vedanta religion and other forms of mysticism would dominate Salinger's life and work.

Salinger's interest in Eastern philosophy and religion started in the late 1940s and continued for the rest of his life. He visited the Ramakrishna-Vivekananda Center in New York, met with other devotees, went on retreats, and devoured sacred Hindu texts. By the time he coaxed Claire to move with him to Cornish, he had already begun to fashion his life according to the principles of Vedanta that stressed simplicity, nature, and spirituality. The two vowed to respect all life including the tiniest of insects and spent their days meditating and practicing yoga and their nights reading religious texts. Sexual abstinence was a part of the Vedanta philosophy and the two rarely had sex since the body, according to Salinger, was the locus of evil. Over his lifetime, Salinger would dabble in Scientology, Zen Buddhism, corporeal procedures such as acupuncture, and macrobiotics, a version of vegetarianism. Clearly, the author was searching for some effective way to deal with his PTSD and his sexual compulsions. Joyce Maynard's description of her life with Salinger decades later would prove similar to Claire's.

One could argue that religion is the driving force in the novel *The Catcher in the Rye*. The reason Holden rails so mercilessly against white culture is because Salinger witnessed the atrocities against primarily Jewish people in Nazi Germany. Religious consciousness dominates the novel but is closeted and hidden. That Salinger essentially devoted his life to spiritual awakening and creating a personal relationship with God magnifies the lack of overt religious contemplation on the part of Holden. The other motivating factor with regard to Salinger and Holden and one that is much more apparent in Holden is his preoccupations with sex, which emerges in the form of various kinds of alternative sexualities presented in the novel, such as homosexuality. These are clearly stand-ins for Salinger's shame regarding his uncontrollable interest in very young girls. Salinger was generally secretive and was uncomfortable in betraying too much of himself through Holden, and so Salinger's obvious preoccupation with religion is muted in Holden since it reflects his wounds and weaknesses. Salinger's preoccupations before, during, and after the novel shed more light on Holden's motivations than anything Holden actually says to the shrink, and it is important to note that Holden does not really say anything of any consequence to anyone but the shrink.

We have no idea what actually happens to Holden Caulfield after the novel *The Catcher in the Rye*, but we do know what happened to Salinger and Elvis. There are a lot of stories out there claiming that Elvis said this or that concerning members of other races. One story suggests that once Elvis said that niggers could only shine his shoes and buy his records. Another story contends that Elvis said he would prefer to kiss multiple African American women rather than just one Mexican woman, implying that he would rather not kiss either one. Both stories seem apocryphal and are not substantiated in any meaningful way. However, the record is pretty clear that Elvis was upset about the prospect of his daughter marrying a nonwhite person.[12] Evidence of Elvis making racist comments complicates our idea of Elvis as an innocent when it comes to his musical debt to black culture. Generally the critical consensus agrees that at the beginning Elvis was a sponge when it came to incorporating black performances into his own act but that later Elvis's style became derivative and packaged. At first, the possibilities for Elvis of racial crossover were endless. Presley had the opportunity to meld southern white and black culture into something that had never been seen. Elvis's cultural emergence dovetailed with the beginning of a civil rights movement that decried blackface minstrelsy, perhaps concomitantly underscoring Elvis's brand of blackness that was about how a body moved opposed to how a body looked. The potential for Presley to capitalize on black sexual stereotypes could have benefited both Presley and African American men and women who were murdered and raped in the name of these stereotypes. Presley did benefit from the overt sexualization of his own body, but because he eventually distanced himself from African Americans, the sexualization of his white body did nothing to dilute the sexual stereotypes that informed the myth of the black rapist or the parallel hypersexualization of black women that rendered them vulnerable to rape.

Elvis's playboy mansion Graceland that he moved into with his parents in 1957 represents perhaps the greatest example of his full embrace of whiteness. We can surmise that Elvis's black influence served a purpose, and once that purpose was achieved, the possibilities of racial crossover ended. Elvis's fame and fortune rendered his obligation to black culture mute. Ironically, once he physically removed himself from black spaces, he was free to explore blackness from the point of view of a racial dabbler rather than a racialized member. Despite Presley growing up around African Americans, he moved into a house in a Memphis suburb aptly named Whitehaven. Elvis and a business partner co-opted the name for one of their business projects. Whitehaven was a developing subdivision and the railroad stop was merely a grassy field with a sign that said "White."

Presley's success and the wealth that he accumulated as well as his physical distancing from African Americans confirmed his whiteness despite his racial roots and influences. By occupying a white space instead of a black one, Presley was less at risk when it came to how he was viewed by the public. Any racial crossover was muted by Graceland, which functioned as a symbol of his allegiance to white privilege regardless of whether Presley felt any different about his formative influences. By removing himself from black culture even while still immersed in it, Elvis avoided any sort of possibility for real race-change. Perhaps a more salient clue in relation to Elvis's feelings about race was that Elvis was absent from the civil rights movement fomenting in his backyard. Another telling fact is Elvis's relationship with perhaps the whitest performer of all time, Frank Sinatra. Based on this narrative, it would seem that Presley's venture out of the closet was short lived and closed off by the fruits of fame. The potential was there, but the allure of success was too powerful. If Holden were to follow the same path as Presley, Holden would have become a corporate lawyer like his father, enjoying the very fruits of privilege that he slammed when he was sixteen. Like Elvis, Salinger retreated back into the closet in order to protect himself from a public who he feared would persecute him for being Jewish and for his unseemly sexual behavior. Salinger simply could not risk persecution, and so, rather than doubling down on his antiestablishment antiwhite sensibilities stemming from the war, he hightailed it back into self-imposed silence and a monastic rejection of the body, coupled with a live-in female teenager.

Elvis's race-change and the concomitant potential for crossover was aborted once Elvis's success allowed him to remove himself from black spaces. In this sense, Elvis was a crossover artist rather than a race-changer. That Elvis early on in his career was ridiculed for being a "white nigger" could have provided him with an opportunity to embrace that status. Elvis grew up around poor blacks and, although his father was around when he was growing up, he was notorious for being often out of work due to his back and generally in the background when it came to family affairs. By all accounts, Elvis's mother ran the household and was the mover and shaker in the family, not unlike many black families whose fathers fall victim to oppression, incarceration, and macho cultural pressure. What Elvis lacked was a racial politics to accompany his impulse to meld white and black cultures.

While Elvis was navigating the racial minefield that would inform his legacy, the 1950s saw *The Catcher in the Rye* go from a novel that was read widely but not entirely embraced as a great book, and in some circles criticized for being overly inflated and exaggerated as an important novel, to a novel that was widely considered an immediate American classic. *The Catcher in the Rye* was first published in July 1951 by Little, Brown and Company and at the same time as a Book-of-the-Month-Club selection. By the end of that first month, Little, Brown and Company had reprinted the novel five times. One month later, the novel rose to fourth place on the *New York Times* best-seller list. The first paperback edition appeared as a Signet Books title in 1953, selling more than three million copies over the following decade. Grosset and Dunlap released their own edition in 1952 and Modern Library released their edition in 1958.[13] Some early reviewers of the novel negatively focused on the narrator. For example, one reviewer believed there was simply too much of the narrator, too much of Holden.[14] Another responded negatively to Holden's potential power to influence young readers.[15] Early on, Holden was viewed as a threat to the social order. What makes him so dangerous is not his violent fantasies or his struggles with formal schooling. These seem like fairly normal issues endemic to teenagers. Rather, what folks likely feared propagating was Holden's unwillingness to subscribe to the hierarchies at play in American culture that ensure an underclass.

Others just simply found the book dull and unsurprising.[16] Still others, on the heels of Salinger's second effort, the book of short stories *Nine Stories*, dismissed *Catcher* as the lesser of the two books.

Nevertheless, by the end of the 1950s, the book enjoyed a host of critics who felt that the novel was an instant classic. Critics began employing timeless literary buzzwords when describing the novel, likening it to a mythic quest for the holy grail and Holden Caulfield as the knight-errant. Framing the novel in these terms aided in transforming it from a noteworthy book from a promising author to a classic. Additionally, Ihab Hassan, in his essay "J. D. Salinger: Rare Quixotic Gesture," etched out the dominant image of Holden Caulfield as a saint that critics held on to into the sixties.[17] These sorts of evaluations lent the character an image of holiness and cool that readers adopted for decades to come. What is clear is that the wide range of critical responses in the first decade of its publication would have in no way foretold of the novel's popularity among readers and its place in American letters nor of the author's notoriousness as a writer who refused to publish or communicate with a public and readership starving for more.

The Cold War sensibility of the 1950s driven by fearmongering in relation to the global threat of communism sparked a phobia of individualism that certainly informed Salinger and paved the way for opportunistic demagogues like Joseph McCarthy. The threat of being branded a communist, a pervert, or someone who was different in any way no doubt fueled both Salinger's and Elvis's eventual decision to go ahead and embrace their whiteness rather than risk their careers and, in the case of Salinger, possibly his reputation and freedom.

The don't-rock-the-boat mood of the 1950s also brought about the first of many censorships of the novel. The first formal record of an attempt to ban the novel occurred in 1954. This attempt and attempts that spanned the following half decade were based on a list of twenty objectionable books. Clearly, readers shared the concerns of some early reviewers that Holden Caulfield represented a sort of catchy virulent worldview that needed to be snuffed out. While these complainants often cited the language in the novel or the references to sexuality, it seems more likely that what they were afraid of was Holden's indictment of an affluent white culture to which people aspired.

The criticism in the 1950s also established some of the arguments that continued on about the book for decades. For example, critics broached the theme of sexuality and homosexuality with regard to Holden and Mr. Antolini,[18] as well as the themes of masculinity[19] and the importance of children.[20] Critics also broached the topic of the novel's frame narrative structure and the fact that Holden is telling his story to a shrink.[21]

Critics would eventually view the book as a harbinger for the counterculture of the 1960s to come and hail it as launching the beat generation several years before Jack Kerouac's *On the Road*.[22] By the end of the decade of the 1950s, *The Catcher in the Rye* was widely considered emblematic of a generation. The alienated youth of the fifties finally found a mouthpiece. Holden rejected stuffy white culture and truly embodied the rebel without a cause before James Dean made the phrase famous.[23]

Salinger's World War II experiences inspired him to write a novel that he could not ultimately live up to because he had too much to hide. He could not make good on his promise to be emblematic of a generation. Despite the novel setting the tone for the next decade, a decade marked by its radical potential for revolution, the 1950s was a decade marred by the intensity with which people feared difference. This fear perhaps prevented Elvis from assuming a race-changing identity that would have seen his legacy grow into one defined by hope instead of tragedy. Like Holden, Elvis scrambled back into the closet rather than embracing the roots that initially informed his music. Elvis could have represented the first hyperfamous cultural race-changer, a global phenomenon endemic to America that capitalized on our roots as a country of inclusion and from which might have sprung sounds and identities the world had never seen. As for Salinger, he had already made up his mind before 1950 that he was not going to be the fountainhead for a country that desperately needed one. The country had the wrong guy. While the public was devouring his novel and book of short stories and hailing him as the voice of a generation, he was totally preoccupied with at once ensuring total access to a young female body and trying desperately to deny himself that access through religious contemplation.

3

CATCHER IN THE SIXTIES
False Profits

Not coincidentally, at the midway point of the decade of the sixties, Salinger decided to quit publishing. This was an era of potential in desperate need of visionary cultural leaders who could lead the way with cultural artifacts and messages at odds with the status quo. In the sixties, like it or not, or deservedly or not, artists, especially musicians, took on ad hoc leadership roles in the various movements. For many African Americans, the black arts movement, spearheaded by a group of vanguard black writers and artists who used art as a means toward revolution, was instrumental in delivering the cultural message that blackness was beautiful, resulting in a discovering, uncloseting, empowering movement that in part resulted in civil rights legislation. For many white people, the sixties was very much about music that had the power to assemble likeminded individuals interested in political change. White people like black people could have also benefited from writers and artists carrying a message of inclusion and love. Salinger and musical groups like the Rolling Stones not only failed to deliver this message but, perhaps more egregiously, failed to provide cultural leadership for a readership and audience from whom they had already financially benefited. Even though Salinger quit producing the kinds of cultural artifacts that functioned as beacons for a hungry fan base ready to mobilize in the name of peace, love, and harmony and all the wonderful ideas yet possible for humanity, his published works, especially *The Catcher in the Rye*, continued to inspire readers at ever-greater numbers as well as scare them. The novel resonated with a white readership who saw in Holden a young person like themselves dissatisfied with a materialistic, white supremacist culture predicated on exclusion and exploitation and identified with his internal war and subsequent clinical unburdening. Simultaneously, the novel spooked other students as well as their parents and became one of the most widely challenged books in the country. Salinger and the Rolling Stones failed a culture who relied on its cultural producers for leadership, and in the case of the Rolling Stones, the result was deadly.

By 1960, Salinger was convinced that he was channeling God in his writing. If this were indeed the case, then clearly God wanted J. D. Salinger to be a rich man. By 1961, *The Catcher in the Rye* had sold 1.25 million copies and continued to sell more than 100,000 copies a year.[1] This combined with the sales for *Franny and Zooey* allowed him to eventually purchase a neighboring plot of land after he caught wind that a trailer park was planned for the space. The author of *The Catcher in the Rye* was appalled with the idea that a trailer park and its occupants would be in such close proximity to his Cornish retreat.[2] Like Elvis, Salinger had moved to his Whitehaven and was not about to allow it to be sullied by trailer trash that might cross his path. Salinger had turned into the very reactionary conservative that Holden would have despised. By purchasing the land that had been slated for a trailer park, Salinger endeared himself to the white people living in the community. To them he was a hero who had ensured that the wrong kind of people would not sully the area. Consequently, these people would protect Salinger from the thousands of people who sought him out over the years by pretending not only that they had no idea where the author lived but that they had no clue of anyone by the name J. D. Salinger. The author to a point had successfully camouflaged himself in a cloud of whiteness.

Along with wanting to have nothing to do with a trailer park next door, Salinger wanted nothing to do with any of the movements gaining momentum in the decade. In 1961, Gordon Lish, the famous editor who had so much influence on the early work of Raymond Carver, was working at the Behavioral Research Laboratories, a California branch of the federal Office of Economic Opportunity. Lish requested that Salinger write a piece that might encourage and instill confidence in unemployed, at-risk, urban youths. Lish's impetus for calling on the author stemmed from his perceived ability to connect with children. Salinger accused Lish of trying to capitalize on Salinger's fame, and when Lish rejoined that Salinger could really talk to children, Salinger retorted that he could not even talk to his own children, much less urban youths.[3] What is striking here is that Lish tried to play up an obvious strength and characteristic of Salinger's writing that he was very likely self-conscious about. Further, the essay was in relation to urban youths, a euphemism for nonwhite youths. The request seized on the linchpin and emotional center of Salinger's writing, and consequently there was no way Salinger was going to open himself up.

In 1961, an article appeared in the *Chicago Tribune* titled "Everybody Gets into Act but Elusive Mr. Salinger." In the article, Harry Hansen noted that despite Salinger's books, including the recently released *Franny and Zooey*, enjoying enormous sales and popularity, no one had been able to interview the author and find out how he achieved his amazing literary effects. Hansen went on to reference a belief that Salinger had notebooks upon notebooks full of fragments of speech that he had overheard, especially the speech of young people ostensibly with whom he often interacted. He also cited a rumor that sometimes Salinger stayed all night at the offices of the *New Yorker*. One paragraph titled "Mysterious Author" claimed that Salinger had been writing since he was fifteen and referenced a newsman who attempted to seek the author out only to return with a meager photograph of a mailbox.[4] Only ten years after *The Catcher in the Rye* came out, the mystique of the Salinger machine was already in motion. Already writers were beginning to grow more interested in the man himself than the work and starting to seek him out in ever-growing numbers.

Perhaps nothing represented the swinging sixties more than the Kennedys. In 1962, the year before the president was assassinated, Kennedy invited Salinger to the White House. Salinger declined because he was worried that the president would press him into public service. Salinger also feared the dinner would be a well-publicized event full of news media. So when Jackie Kennedy called him on the phone inviting him to the dinner, he said very little to the first lady, making it clear that he would not attend.[5] What sort of public service did Salinger fear? No doubt in 1962 the president was very concerned with the ongoing civil rights movement. Just one year later Kennedy would propose the Civil Rights Act of 1964. Kennedy likely thought Salinger might be interested in taking part in the movement.

Along with a fomenting political landscape erupting across the country during the sixties, the decade is often associated with the politically driven music that functioned as much more than the soundtrack to the Age of Aquarius. The impression is that the music and politics were birds of a feather, symbiotically vital to either's existence. If this were true, then one has to wonder why the end of the sixties supposedly occurred at a rock concert forty miles away from the epicenter of the Age of Aquarius, San Francisco, while one of the members of the age's royalty sang that he hoped everything would be all right. What is more likely true is that the death of Meredith Hunter at the Altamont Free Rock Festival on December 6, 1969, dispelled the illusion that in the sixties musicians were able or even willing to usher in an era of love and inclusivity.

The idea that the Altamont Free Rock Festival ended the sixties revolves around a member of the Hells Angels killing of a black man named Meredith Hunter. The implication baked into this narrative is that there never really was such a sixties to begin with that a racialized hate killing could have dashed. Often Woodstock is offered as an example of the obverse of Altamont, but Woodstock only occurred about three months earlier. That two cultural occurrences happening three months apart can represent symbolic bookends to an entire decade amounts to little more than an absurdity and calls into question the decade's reputation as a time of idealistic possibility. As Todd Gitlin relates,

> The tale has been told many times of how, at Altamont, among three hundred thousand fans, the Hells Angels, serving as semiofficial guards, killed a young fan, black, who had a white date and the temerity to offend the Angels (by getting too close to them, or their motorcycles, or the stage), and then, at some point, pulled a gun—all the while Mick Jagger was singing "Under My Thumb." . . . [The] effect was to burst the bubble of youth culture's illusions about itself. Who could any longer harbor the illusion that these hundreds of thousands of spoiled star-hungry children of the Lonely Crowd were the harbingers of a good society?[6]

Among the many misconceptions that led to the death of Meredith Hunter was that Mick Jagger and the Rolling Stones harbored any sort of politics that jibed with the big ideas being thrown around in the counterculture in relation to economic and racial equality. Mick Jagger admitted as much when he said that his song "Street Fighting Man" was not about wanting to join protesters in the streets but rather was about having the freedom to be a rock-and-roll band irrespective of politics.

Like Elvis, the Rolling Stones had the potential to be the harbingers of a new era, the potential to double bounce off their African American musical influences and actually lead the way with their music to an era of racial and economic inclusivity. They were just not interested. Where Elvis was a racial exploiter of African American music, too afraid to come out of his closet because of the risk to his fame, money, and privilege, the Rolling Stones were race betrayers who existed under the illusive aegis of a politics they did not actively support. Holden Caulfield, Elvis, and the Rolling Stones all could have embraced their latent roles as racial change agents, could have exited the white racial closet, leaving a positive racial legacy in their wake. The Rolling Stones' decision to disavow this built-in potential got a black man killed at one of their own concerts.

Just five months prior to Altamont, the Stones gave a free concert in Hyde Park, London, employing what the band thought was a group of UK bikers affiliated with the California-based biker gang the Hells Angels. Never mind that this British version of the Hells Angels was a far cry from the real California-based biker gang or that their outfits were festooned with Nazi symbolism. Where exactly in the Age of Aquarius does the swastika fit in? Perhaps these were Hells Angels light. Maybe they were not the real deal, but if they were similar enough, chances are that casual similarity included a shared white supremacist ideology. If the Stones were even remotely involved in the politics associated with the new world the hippies promised, then surely Nazi iconography would not have been allowed. The truth is the Stones likely did not even notice the Nazi symbols shrouded around the backs of those they put in charge. These were their authority figures. This was the ideological state apparatus at the concert. They would also be present at Altamont where, as everyone knew, evidently except the Rolling Stones, the California-based Hells Angels were known for being reactionary white supremacists and were a hell of a lot more serious than the posers in London who had to be home for dinner right after the concert.

Even though the Rolling Stones did not grow up around southern American black people, like Elvis, and perhaps because of Elvis, the Stones' music was heavily influenced by the same southern black blues that Elvis's was. Keith Richards cites Elvis as a gateway musician along with the black artists who influenced Elvis.[7] The other members of the Stones claimed an interest in African American culture as well, especially music. Bill Wyman admits that seeing Chuck Berry in *Rock, Rock, Rock* gave him the music bug. Keith Richards loved the movie as well. When Mick Jagger and Keith Richards first met at the Dartford train station, Mick had a Chuck Berry record under his arm. The two bumped into one another and soon decided to meet up.[8]

Elvis's lack of racial politics and decision to not take part in the civil rights movement paved the way for future white artists to exploit African American music without an accompanying racial politics demonstrating that borrowing from African Americans necessitated a concomitant valuing of the lives of African Americans in addition to admiring the culture. Had Elvis honored his roots both in relation to place and music, consistently kept his influences in mind, and embraced his racial roots as a necessary identity in relation to his music, then perhaps other artists would have followed suit. Elvis could have established a norm of etiquette or an unwritten code within the music industry that demanded that if one was going to borrow music from African Americans, then one needed to support the cause of racial equality. This did not happen.

During the tour that would culminate in the free concert at Altamont Speedway, the Stones performed their African American–influenced rock. The Stones often played covers written by black artists such as Chuck Berry and Robert Johnson, yet they did not couple this illustration of cultural fusion with a racial politics allergic to security sporting Nazi paraphernalia. Since music was so vital in the sixties, it was especially important for musicians to be politically engaged, even on a very superficial level. Unfortunately, the Rolling Stones viewed American politics and the racial strife going on in the streets as a mere nuisance that put a damper on an otherwise high time. The political nuisance the Stones found annoying in the late 1960s was very much racially laden. Just one year prior, Martin Luther King was shot to death in Memphis, resulting in riots all over the country. The fans who attended the concerts in the sixties and who bought the records from the bands capitalizing on the politics of the day had every right to expect their rock heroes to care about racial equality, especially since they owed a great debt to the very group that was experiencing so much injustice. One could not expect to avoid racial violence when it was inconvenient and then ride the wave of the popular struggle that resulted from it when it was commercially valuable. Despite American politics dogging the tour, there was no way to avoid it since concertgoers looked to the music to carry the message. Because music was the epicenter of the 1960s, there was no way the Stones could have avoided the racial problems of the 1960s. What made them think they were immune? The lack of political engagement on behalf of the Stones calls into question all the big ideas that the 1960s were supposed to represent. An attitude divorced from any sort of real political engagement is useless.

One of many ironies in the death of Meredith Hunter is that he was killed by ad hoc racist law enforcement appointed by the Rolling Stones because the Stones felt that the real law enforcement was not to be trusted since they had demonstrated a lack of tolerance for a counterculture that in part demanded racial equality. In other words, the Stones hired a racist biker gang as security since they felt that real cops were too racist. In England by 1969, the Stones had conflicted with the police on many occasions. To them, the police were part of the problem rather than part of the solution. Consequently, while they still needed security at their concerts, they were not interested in off-duty police officers acting as security at their shows since they did not trust the English police. As far as the cops in the United States, the Stones were very familiar with the images of throngs of helmeted police beating protesters at the 1968 Democratic National Convention. They had also seen the nasty images of conflicts between civil rights marchers and police, especially in the South. They needed security, but it could not be the regular cops in either country.[9]

Salinger's last published work, *Hapworth 16, 1924*, appeared in the *New Yorker* in 1965 and was universally panned by critics as totally unreadable. The novella would appear in the next decade in a pirated copy of Salinger's uncollected short stories. It seems fitting that the last anyone heard from Salinger was in the sixties, perhaps the decade with the most potential for change in relation to popular struggle.

After 1965, Salinger ceased to be a producer of cultural artifacts, but he did not cease to be a part of the culture. Through his silence he became a cultural artifact himself. Readers no longer had any writing of his to read and consume, so they read and consumed the man as best they could. Salinger had produced cultural artifacts, especially *The Catcher in the Rye*, that rather than affirming a stifling culture was at odds with it. It seems that he spent most of his time after publishing the novel trying to take it all back. *The Catcher in the Rye* as a cultural artifact did not provide a means of escape for the drone working man in the fifties to consume and thereby forget his sorry lot in life. To the contrary, the book questioned and ultimately condemned the universally agreed upon American definition of success and the ideal life also known as the American dream. Holden attacks materialism, white supremacy, and all manner of normativity. Once Salinger published the book, it took on a life of its own, invigorated by life-giving readers who either embraced it as revolutionary or rejected it as dangerous to the status quo. It is very hard to argue that the book lacked the power its readers clearly felt it contained. Once Salinger quit publishing, *The Catcher in the Rye* and his other works did not die. The artifacts continued to move through history, occupying a biography of their own. What seems clear is that Salinger no longer wished to produce cultural artifacts that contained the sort of power that required that he relinquish control. He had too much to hide, was too comfortable in the tug-of-war going on in his own psyche that featured religious renunciation on one end and young girls on the other. For a man who guarded his privacy so dearly, he had created the biggest blabbermouths one can imagine, his own books that would never shut up. There was no way to shut them up. And they had plenty to say. The unfortunate part of Salinger's silence is the fact that he did not have the courage to attempt to create more artifacts at odds with a culture ripe for change. There is no way to know whether he would have written anything that inspired readers like *The Catcher in the Rye* did. Most of his other work seems to be more about himself than anything else, more revealing about the man and his hang-ups than indictments of venal white America. Once we are able to view his posthumous works, if and when they are released and if they even exist, we will know. Ironically, once readers had exhausted his oeuvre, they turned to the very thing he wanted to avoid: they began to read the man. Salinger became the primary artifact that his adoring fans read and his every move was a new page to be consumed by that hungry public.

The Stones did not want the men in blue working security at their concerts due to their association with confrontations with civil rights marches. So instead, they hired a known racist group who incorporated Nazi symbolism, including the swastika, in their enforcement attire. One member of the Rolling Stones' entourage at Altamont described the Hells Angels as "very spooky. The whole energy was truly awful. . . . The Hells

Angels always scared me. I knew, of course, about their peaceful reputation in the San Francisco scene. I'd read how Ken Kesey invited them to participate, and how they would stand next to the stage at concerts in San Francisco, a kind of unofficial security presence—an example of the inclusiveness of the new Aquarian world order. Still, I was nervous. It felt uncomfortable."[10] To some, the supposed assimilation of the Hells Angels into the hippie scene actually represented a form of diversity, indicating a positive step in the direction of inclusiveness. This reminds one of the assimilation of the Irish in the mid-nineteenth century who earned their whiteness by infiltrating the ranks of law enforcement and brutally defending white supremacy. Evidently for Kesey and for the Rolling Stones, extending an olive branch to a known violent and racist biker gang to take part in the new world order was more important than actually extending an olive branch to minorities who would actually benefit from it.

Once firmly ensconced at Altamont as authority figures, it did not take long for the Angels to prove themselves unfit for their role. There were reports that before the concert, in some cases by other musicians, the Angels were already out of control. Prior to the first band tuning their instruments, Michelle Phillips of the Mamas and the Papas told the Stones' entourage that the Angels were working for beer and had been throwing full cans at people as well as ingesting large amounts of LSD provided for free by Augustus Owsley Stanley III. These chilling descriptions of the folks who were supposed to be in charge transcended the brutality, abuse, and corruption of the real police since the Angels were hired by the Rolling Stones, who were trusted to represent the vision of the youth movement.

The Rolling Stones not only betrayed concertgoers with their apathy and carelessness; they also betrayed themselves and the other bands. At one point during the concert a member of the Hells Angels security force knocked out the lead singer of Jefferson Airplane. The idea that an Angel would attack the very people he was supposed to protect highlights the absurdity in hiring such a group. These were folks who could not be trusted. The real blame should be placed on the shoulders of the men who made the decision to hire a violent hate group as an ideological state apparatus to defend an ideology that the Stones did not even really believe in but only profited from when it was financially advantageous to do so.

Tony Funches, an African American bodyguard on tour with the Stones that summer, revealed, "So it starts and I'm watching it go down. There's these two Hells Angels having a fight with each other just before the Airplane went on. I ask 'em to take the fight somewhere else, because they are messing up the stage. They look at me with pinwheel eyes going, and my lizard brain got ready for combat. One guy says, 'I ain't taking no orders from no nigger.'"[11]

The notion that Altamont ended the sixties assumes that the sixties were actually about real change. Altamont exposed the hypocrisy and real consequences for disaffected youth inherent in the 1960s. Despite Altamont taking place only three months after Woodstock, the two concerts have a completely different symbolism; one functions as a symbol of the potential for the counterculture and the other a symbol for its hopelessness and fraudulence. How can they both be true?

I would argue that Altamont is the more accurate reflection of the reality of the 1960s, particularly in relation to musicians functioning as change agents. The contrast between the concerts was apparent from the start. Famously, right after Mick Jagger emerged from his helicopter on the grounds of Altamont, a stoned fan punched him in the face. Ostensibly a member of the audience punched what he had come to see, similar to security going after that which they have been employed to secure.

The Altamont Speedway was a desolate area east of San Francisco. Unlike Woodstock, Altamont felt perfunctory and performed, lacking the sort of authenticity that made Woodstock seem extemporaneous, off the cuff, a happy accident. One explanation might be that the optimism and energy in the early part of the youth and hippie movement had carried a lot of the members, but that by the time Altamont happened there were lots of youth who were sort of just along for the ride and who were taking part in the drug culture more so than the political culture. This explanation would be reasonable if Woodstock had not occurred just two handfuls of weeks earlier. In fact, there is a good chance that all the *really weird hippies* hanging around Altamont were the same really weird hippies that were at Woodstock. These were many of the same displaced impressionable kids who were on the East Coast the previous summer looking to musicians for political guidance and being failed miserably. The truth is that Woodstock was the illusion and Altamont was the reality.

The bad vibes of Altamont combined with the hiring of a white supremacist biker gang as security culminated in a hate crime that illustrated the folly in looking to opportunistic racial exploiters and betrayers as
anything but a stage show. The victim of that hate crime was Meredith
Hunter, an eighteen-year-old black man from Oakland. He had driven to
the concert in his black Mustang with his seventeen-year-old white girlfriend, Patty Bredehoft. Once violence broke out at the concert, Hunter
returned to his car and retrieved his long-barreled .22 caliber pistol, stuck
it into his waistband, and returned to Bredehoft. The two then made their
way to the stage as the Stones prepared to perform.[12] No one knows
exactly what took place in front of the stage. The accepted story is that
Hunter drew his gun and was stabbed to death by Alan Passaro, a Hells
Angel. This act was the equivalent of a mob lynching. Passaro repeatedly
stabbed Meredith Hunter in the back with a big knife. In this respect,
Passaro acted as judge, jury, and executioner, proving his assimilation
into the hippie scene by brutalizing what he viewed as an interloper just
as the Irish did in the mid-nineteenth century. This was the equivalent of
a Jim Crow–style kangaroo court in the span of about thirty seconds,
whereby the judge, jury, and executioner were all white racists. Hunter
never had a chance. Perhaps he did draw his gun. Perhaps he even meant
to harm the band like one Angel already had. But this act could have been
thwarted without murdering the man. Because this man was black, he was
not given a chance; he was not afforded his day in court. He was simply
killed like a runaway slave.

Eventually Passaro, the very likely drunk and tripping Hells Angel
who repeatedly stabbed Hunter, was put on trial and subsequently acquit-
ted of any wrongdoing. Passaro's defense centered on the argument that
Hunter had a gun and had pointed it at the stage. This moment in question
is captured in footage shot by Albert and David Maysles that would later
be used in the documentary film *Gimme Shelter* (1970), chronicling the
last weeks of the tour. The film is grainy and blurry and it is hard to tell
where Hunter pointed his gun or if he pointed it at all. It appears as
though he raises it, but at whom and for what purpose is unclear. What we
do know is that night Hunter was very likely the hunted rather than the
hunter. The idea that Passaro saved the life of Mick Jagger is pure specu-
lation and a ridiculous historical revision underscoring the idea that history is often written by those in power. No one took responsibility for

Hunter's death. The victim took the blame despite the obvious absurdity of the Hells Angels acting as law enforcement.

The idealistic intentions of a generation flew off the cliff because there was no catcher in the rye to catch them, no real change maker or race-changer to lead the way. The Rolling Stones certainly were not up to the task, and yet, the musicians were the ones entrusted to lead this excitable generation. This was a wasted opportunity. The spirit of the sixties did not peak and wane in the span of ninety days. There never was any freedom and there was very little love. All else was a stoned illusion.

In 1960, *The Catcher in the Rye* had been out for nine years and Salinger was living the life of a recluse in New Hampshire. The decade would bring about his last and final three published works: *Franny and Zooey*; *Raise High the Roof Beam, Carpenters and Seymour: An Intro-duction*; and *Hapworth 16, 1924*. Early in the decade famed director Elia Kazan supposedly cornered Salinger in New York and begged the author to allow the director the opportunity to stage *Catcher* on Broadway. Sal-inger's response was that he feared Holden would not approve.[13] This response is revealing in that it attributes the responsibility for the novel to Holden and not the author. Also, early in the decade *Newsweek* published a story about Salinger, noting that he was a registered Republican and hence was very likely a Nixon man during the 1960 election.[14] This fact perhaps should not come as a surprise considering Salinger's reluctance to get involved in the counterculture in any way despite the general feel-ing that his character Holden Caulfield anticipated the cultural dissatis-faction characteristic of the decade and notwithstanding his experiences in war. No, by the sixties, Salinger wanted no part of free love and communal living outside of his Cornish retreat, and evidently was too afraid of his sexual activities becoming public to speak out against the horrors of war or for civil rights.

Critically, the sixties marked a coming-out party for *The Catcher in the Rye*, Holden Caulfield, and Salinger as the author of the text. The hagiographic treatment of Holden Caulfield developed organically among sixties college students. If there was a good sixties, or the potential for a good sixties, it was in relation to the politically minded students of all races and genders demonstrating against the war and questioning the curriculum on campuses all over the country that ultimately led to new programs such as African studies and women's, gender, and sexuality studies. Holden Caulfield particularly spoke to this generation because of his indictment of the power structure responsible for the inequities that marked the American class and culture system. A more cynical view would hold that Holden resonated with a faction of the population whose political and radical feelings existed in the closet and that they found in the character a kindred soul walking around internally at war but externally very sick. Nevertheless, as Pamela Hunt Steinle notes,

> Ten years after the initial publication of *The Catcher in the Rye* . . . many bookstores . . . reported it among their most-wanted paperbacks. . . . Between 1959 and 1963, at least twenty scholarly essays were devoted to *The Catcher in the Rye*. . . . The popularity of *The Catcher in the Rye* among American youth and particularly college students was extravagant, leading Laser and Fruman to comment that "observers of the American scene know that Salinger is by far the most popular author, living or dead, among college students."[15]

As the novel grew in popularity over the decade, so did its author. By the end of the decade Salinger was regarded as one of the very best authors in the United States.

As college students were identifying with Holden Caulfield and his indictment of phony white culture, a powerful faction in America viewed the book as dangerous and worthy of destruction. For example, in April of 1961, a student at the University of Texas formally complained about *Catcher* being part of the required reading list for her second-year English course. When the university supported the professor who assigned the book on the syllabus, the student's father, a Houston attorney and port commissioner, threatened to withdraw his daughter from the school.

The history of *The Catcher in the Rye* in the 1960s is a parallel history. On one hand, the book was the most popular book in the United States among college students and perhaps the most demonized among parents, especially of high schoolers, demarcating the generational gap between the youth of the sixties and the baby boomers coming of age in the fifties. In 1963, the American Book Publishers Council declared *Catcher* the most consistently "damned" book in the entire country.[16] The bifurcated history of the novel in the sixties speaks to a fractured culture wherein youth saw in Holden an example of rhetoric with no clear political program and parents saw the same thing.

Eve Sedgwick once referenced black people coming out of the closet as black in the sixties.[17] She meant that in the sixties black people owned their blackness not by fighting an interior war or hiding from political engagement but by making their war public through a political and artistic program. If that is so, then unfortunately white people have never come out or even acknowledged whiteness as anything but normal and raceless. The sixties was a decade where the door became ajar and white folks could have come out of the closet as openly against white supremacy. People were pining to come out of the closet, and some certainly did. Throngs of people across America were certainly talking about coming out of the closet, getting high and talking about it.

As the civil rights movement raged on, *The Catcher in the Rye* enjoyed unparalleled popularity among college students. They saw in Holden a person like themselves, upset at the inequities of the social order and yet impotent at the same time. While many gains were made in the civil rights and black power movements and the women's movement, like Holden, essentially white Americans stayed in the closet, unbeckoned by the false idols of the decade like the Rolling Stones, who, while capitalizing on the energy and spirit of the decade, refused to embrace the politics and truly lead. Like Holden and Elvis, the Rolling Stones could have emerged from the racial closet and embraced a multicultural identity that could have been the standard bearer, but like Salinger they said no and passed up on the opportunity to truly make a difference. It is not a surprise that in 2010 the FBI admitted that it had never kept a file on Salinger in an era when writers were often surveilled and had files, such as James Baldwin, Ernest Hemingway, and Norman Mailer. The *Toronto Star* noted that even though *The Catcher in the Rye* criticized phonies and the white power structure and was often cited as a seminal text in the counterculture movement, Salinger was not politically active and so therefore there was no need to keep a file on him. [18]

The popularity of the novel and Holden in particular in the decade, then, can be viewed as somewhat alarming. *The Catcher in the Rye* presented a rebel in the closet talking to a shrink. In no way is Holden Caulfield a political activist. Holden is fearful of being found out. He is not ready to truly come out of the closet as a nonwhite, as someone who truly identifies with the marginal, as a true catcher in the rye for those who truly need a catcher in the rye. Holden is a safe model to emulate. By the end of the novel, he has not really risked anything that might have a lasting effect. He has not given up his ghost in any way. In fact, he is on the mend and in the process of shutting the closet door. The popularity of the novel among white college students in the sixties speaks to the self-conscious recognition that the book represents bluster with no action. The book signifies a youthful idealism that students can eventually grow out of and get on with the business of making money. Indeed, the seventies marked the decade in which these same college students put away their childish things, including *The Catcher in the Rye*. If there ever was a decade in need of several catchers in the rye standing at cliffs in hopes of saving young people from falling off, it was the sixties. The natural catchers in the rye of the era were the cultural producers who already had the respect and attention of the young people, but alas both Salinger and the Stones just let young people fall.

4

CATCHER IN THE SEVENTIES
Uprisings and Infiltrations

The winds of change that blew wildly in the sixties had not totally died down by the early 1970s. For Salinger, the decade was the first in which he would not publish a thing. While I do not want to argue that new work by the author would have turned the tide of events such as the Attica prison uprising and saved lives, millions of fans had already proven that perhaps, more than any other author, Salinger did have their attention. In light of the events of the decade that required cultural leadership, Salinger's deafening silence became all the more strikingly egregious, especially when juxtaposed with men like William Kunstler who devoted their lives to combatting racial inequality. The legacy of Salinger in the decade of the seventies and his novel *The Catcher in the Rye* pivots on the intensity with which he hid from his fans within a closet of fear and resentment, so much so that reading his work became a crime. The beginning of the decade would shine a light on actual prisons and the growing sense that America was dealing with its racial problems by locking up black people, especially black people who had taken part in the change movements of the previous decade. Focusing on the explosion of the U.S. industrial prison complex in the seventies, in which the United States hid its racial legacy, in juxtaposition with the prison in which Salinger locked himself up against a public hungry for his leadership underscores the glare of his absence from the fractured cultural landscape.

Less than two years after the Rolling Stones held their tragic free concert at the Altamont Speedway, where Meredith Hunter was murdered by a racist and drunken Hells Angel, on September 9, 1971, one thousand of the more than two thousand prisoners in upstate New York's Attica Correctional Facility took over the prison and demanded more humane treatment. In Göran Olsson's documentary *Black Power Mixtape*, the narrator notes, "The prisoners . . . barricaded themselves with 38 guards as hostages . . . [producing] a list of 38 demands for better living conditions in exchange for the hostages. The demands were . . . for more humane treatment, an end of physical abuse, for basic necessities like tooth brushes and showers every day, for professional training and access to newspapers and books, and . . . to [be transported] out of the country to a non-imperialist nation."[1] In part, the uprising was due to Soledad Brother George Jackson being shot to death by correctional officers in San Quentin Prison. Many of the prisoners were leaders and organizers plucked straight out of the civil rights and black power movements, activists very aware of the changing political climate in the American cultural landscape. To make prisoners aware of what was going on outside the prison walls, classes were held in the prison yards. Just before the uprising, guards were particularly unnerved when the prisoners took a vow of silence during their meals, displaying solidarity and organization.

The uprising lasted for four days until the police and National Guardsmen stormed the prison and indiscriminately killed forty people, including thirty-one prisoners and nine guards. Initial reports suggested that the prisoners slit the throats of the nine guards, but eventually autopsies showed that all the people who were killed were killed by the storming troops.

In April of 1972, J. D. Salinger came across a *New York Times* article titled "An Eighteen Year Old Looks Back on Life" written by Yale freshman Joyce Maynard, who was pictured along with the article looking wide eyed, pretty, and girlish.[2] Salinger, who had a habit of contacting very young women whom he encountered through television and the media, was naturally intrigued by this very young and very cute, budding, successful, Ivy League writer. Though a promising writer and intellectual, Joyce was the daughter of a severe alcoholic, not unlike Oona, and had struggled for many years with eating disorders.[3] She melted when she received a long letter from the fifty-three-year-old author of *The Catcher in the Rye*. The two corresponded for some months, and eventually Joyce dropped out of Yale and came to live with Salinger in Cornish like Claire Douglas before her. The relationship only lasted ten months and was complicated by Salinger's refusal to have any more children. Twenty-six years later Maynard would publish her memoirs wherein she accused the author of taking advantage of a young impressionable girl.[4] During the decade there would be more than one human being who attempted to penetrate the prison in which the famous author lived. Salinger initiated the attempt by Maynard. Most of the other attempts were unwelcome. Salinger was both stalker and stalked.

Attica was an explosive racial situation wherein most of the inmates were black and all the guards were white. The racial makeup of the prison as well as the prison itself represented a troubling development in American culture wherein oppressive racial dynamics played out in a space hidden from the American public. In effect, the U.S. industrial prison complex represented a literal national closet in which our racial legacy of abuse lay. While prison has become deeply embedded in our culture, for most people it is at the same time absent from their lives and very easy to ignore. The realities of prison for most people are based on movies and media depictions of prisoners who are unfit for society, when in reality prisons are a form of neo-slavery and evidence of the vast racial problems in the United States.

Prisons allow cultural problems and inequities to go on unsolved; they are a blanket reaction to problems no one wishes to deal with. As a result, prison becomes a deus ex machina for racial as well as capitalistic problems at play since slavery. In a postcolonial situation where a group of people exists in a state of disenfranchisement and economic exclusion and reacts to that situation in kind, hiding them in cages does not represent a sustainable solution to the cause of the problem that set the conflict in motion to begin with. Prison therefore becomes a consequence of inaction and a false and potentially explosive panacea for social problems.

The convict lease system was a way for the United States to maintain its labor power that was once provided by slavery. After slavery, state and local prisons snatched up former slaves for a whole host of contrived reasons and leased them out, sometimes to the very plantations on which they worked as slaves. Often these former slaves were put on chain gangs where their human value was even less than it was as a slave. Often these prisoners of the state were literally worked to death. The idea of prisons for profit, coupled with the fact that the majority of prisoners in the United States are black, reflects a horrific reality in our country whereby black people represent a valuable incarcerated labor force reminiscent of slavery and the convict lease system. Despite private prisons only constituting a small slice of prisons in the United States, the private prison model has proliferated in many countries around the world and has become the fastest growing global development in the penal industry.

In August 2016 the Department of Justice released a statement declaring its intention of scaling back private prisons, citing an intensive investigation and report that indicated that private prisons did not save money and were inferior in almost every way. For-profit prisons are not that much different from public prisons since American businesses profit greatly from public prisons. For example, many food manufacturers, such as Nestlé, provide their products within the prisons for the inmates, guards, and prison staff to buy. The insidiousness of prisons is based largely on its hidden, almost secret existence.

Prison reform falls into the category of ideological impossibility, like abolition movements in the past such as emancipation and desegregation. In this sense, one needs to couple critical thinking with activism in order to make prison reform a reality. The interiority of the industrial prison complex prevents public engagement. Just as Holden's beef with the culture was restricted to his shrink, prisons primarily exist in the public popular imagination while the reality exists in a national closet.

In 1974 some fans decided to take matters into their own hands in relation to Salinger's uncollected cultural artifacts and began peddling two volumes of his uncollected stories in San Francisco, Chicago, and New York. These men, who were referred to as intellectual hippie types and all went by the name John Greenberg, were representative of the very readership that Salinger had left high and dry the previous decade when he decided to quit publishing. The group of renegade hippie Salinger fans printed more than twenty-five thousand copies and sold them like hotcakes to bookstore retailers.[5] At this point, Salinger spent much of his time fortifying his closet and preventing his readers from accessing his work. Because Salinger wanted to avoid a trial, he contacted the *New York Times* and explained his intent to legally prevent the distribution of his uncollected work in hopes of scaring off the booksellers, whom he threatened with massive financial liability. The *New York Times* in response requested an interview with the famous reclusive author who had exchanged his body for his books as the only legible access point for a rabid public forced to go cold turkey in relation to new work by the author of *The Catcher in the Rye*. The interview was conducted by Lacey Fosburgh and, even though Salinger warned her up front over the phone that he only intended to talk for a minute, the interview lasted a half hour.[6] Salinger confirmed that he was still writing but that he had no intention of publishing and felt at peace with his decision. The result was that the *New York Times* article had the effect Salinger hoped for and the books the intellectual hippies were peddling vanished from the shelves. While the distribution of the pirated copies of Salinger's uncollected short stories does constitute a crime and certainly a profit motive for the John Greenbergs, in part the crime was driven by the desire on the part of the public to read more of Salinger's work, in this case older work that had until that point been unavailable or very difficult to find. The distribution of bootleg copies of his work on the black market was the natural consequence of Salinger's decision not to publish. The notion that readers were committing a crime by reading Salinger's work demonstrated the extent to which Salinger had turned his back on the very readers who had made him a wealthy man capable of fully turning his back on them. That same year, the *Chicago Tribune* published an article called "Special Campus Reading Issue" wherein they surveyed students from ninety-one colleges in Illinois and the surrounding five states, asking them what books they were reading that were not required by their professors in their regular classes. *The Catcher in the Rye* ranked number nine on the list. One of the questions on the survey asked not only what the respondent was reading but also what the respondent felt others were reading outside of class work. This suggests that *Catcher* was not only being read by thousands of students but that thousands of students thought others were reading it as well.[7]

One man who did not turn his back on the public and did his best to be a catcher in the rye for folks who needed one and who coupled activism with critical thinking during the Attica prison uprising was William Kunstler, a lawyer, present during the revolt as a member of the observer committee. Kunstler tried to orchestrate negotiations between the prisoners and the authorities led by New York governor Nelson Rockefeller. In *Black Power Mixtape* Kunstler says of the bloodbath that followed the negotiations:

It's murder under any doctrine of civilized standards that any country has ever had. . . . Prisoners had two non-negotiable demands, the removal of the warden and general amnesty. And they had already given up on the removal of the warden. And on the general amnesty, we had worked out several formulas that we were discussing with the commissioner hours before the attack. If we had been allowed to continue, everyone would be alive and the matter would be settled today. [8]

Kunstler at one point admitted that he feared for his life and offered, "Well, I guess I'm a white middle class citizen of this country and I had all the stereotypes about prisoners that any person of my capacity has. I had to learn the hard way that they were decent honorable men, much more decent and much more honorable than the men who went in there to shoot them." [9] This admission is particularly interesting for our purposes in that it illustrates someone acting as a race-changer despite his preconceived racial ideas about a group of marginalized human beings. Even though Kunstler was already considered a radical lawyer sympathetic with racial inequalities, he himself admitted that he still harbored racist stereotypes about black men in prison. It took him to actually engage with the men to realize that they were honorable men and break the stronghold of his assumptions. It took action on his part. In order to make any sort of difference and act on his critical realizations, he had to betray his own race that had a vested economic interest in keeping black prisoners in prison. Kunstler demonstrated the process by which one becomes a change agent or a catcher in the rye. The only problem is that his transformation was too little too late.

Originally on an observer committee, once William Kunstler arrived at Attica during the uprising, he soon agreed to represent the inmates himself. [10] The inmates constructed a list of immediate demands, one of which was demanding Kunstler's services as their legal representative. As Heather Ann Thompson notes, "A graduate of Yale and Columbia, Kunstler was respected both as someone who had served in the Pacific Theater during World War II and as someone who had long been committed to a fiery defense for activists in numerous high-profile civil rights and social justice cases." [11] Like Salinger, Kunstler served in World War II and clearly emerged from that war dedicated to racial equality. Unlike Salinger, Kunstler continued the fight.

Before Kunstler could begin the negotiations with the other lawyers and legal representatives, he had to sign a waiver giving up his or his family's right to hold the state of New York liable should he get hurt.[12] Kunstler had to transcend his fear and the socialized stereotypes that he harbored about black male prisoners. Despite making progress with the negotiations, eventually the state decided to take over the prison with force and indiscriminately butcher anyone they saw. After the prison was stormed by New York storm troopers, Kunstler, who was lucky to have been away from the prison that day, was nearly run down by a car full of men who clearly viewed him as the enemy, a nonwhite hostile combatant. As Kunstler waited to hear about what he feared had taken place, all he could do was sit alone and cry.[13]

Kunstler's experience within Attica demonstrated the difficulty in abandoning one's race in favor of the human race. He witnessed firsthand the hostility and danger involved in becoming a race-changer. Those men who nearly ran him down viewed him as a betrayer of the white race despite the clearly good intentions that he demonstrated. The prisoners at Attica sensed that in Kunstler they had an ally. He would go on to represent John Hill, who was charged with killing one of the guards at Attica. Kunstler would prove to be unsuccessful but once again showed his willingness to catch someone who had been persecuted and marginalized from falling off the cliff.

Salinger's radio silence and the resulting attempts by adoring fans to penetrate the man, to read the man, and to recover what they felt they were missing from their lives caused odd rumors to swirl about. The effect that Salinger had on a readership and his subsequent denial of that effect was similar to an addict abruptly quitting using substances. Fans were addicted and, like many addicts, they went through a period of withdrawal that resulted in irrational behavior and illusory wish fulfillments. One of the oddest to catch fire was the idea that the famous and reclusive writer Thomas Pynchon, author of works like *V*, *Gravity's Rainbow*, and *The Crying of Lot 49*, was in fact Salinger. The rumor began in April 1976 when John Calvin Batchelor published an article in the *Soho Weekly* claiming that Thomas Pynchon's most famous works were actually written by Salinger.[14] The argument was that Salinger hit a dead end with the Glass family and the Caulfields and needed a clean slate on which to create new worlds. Batchelor argued that it was no mere coincidence that Pynchon's first publication appeared in 1965 when Salinger supposedly retired. A public jonesing for more Salinger immediately picked up on the article and the rumor caught fire. Once Pynchon, who like Salinger notoriously guarded his privacy and refused to have his picture taken, wrote to Batchelor refuting his claims, Batchelor had to reevaluate his thesis.

The Pynchon claim was problematic on a number of levels. First off, the notion that Salinger had exhausted the Glass family or even the Caulfield family does not take into consideration the breadth of that world. Salinger's published work is illustrative of Hemingway's iceberg theory. What is visible is only the tip. Secondly, Salinger never had a problem with his worlds; he had a problem with the readership and the reaction his work elicited. The difficulty was in the reveal, and that reveal would be no less apparent in work with a different pen name that might come back to haunt the actual author. Salinger simply could not write without betraying information about himself that he was not comfortable sharing. Great writing required an honesty that Salinger was not willing to offer the public. A different pen name would not have alleviated that fear. Further, at no point did Salinger ever demonstrate the sort of postmodern playfulness found in Pynchon's work. If anything, merely a few strands of Pynchon's many-tentacled dialogic writing resembles Salinger. What drove the comparison was a wish-fulfilling illusion. Batchelor wanted it to be true and so looked beyond obvious reasons why it was not.

In 1978, Michael Clarkson, a police beat reporter from the *Niagara Falls Review*, hopped in his car and left his family and job to seek out the author. After Clarkson found Salinger and confirmed that the author was the man who wrote all the books that he loved, Salinger asked Clarkson what he could do for him. Clarkson told Salinger he did not know and perhaps the author might know. Upon hearing this and finding out the man was a reporter, Salinger abruptly left. Salinger inexplicably returned minutes later and the man then read him a note that he had written asking Salinger for writing advice. Salinger told Clarkson that no man can say anything of any use to any other man and that his decision to seek out the author was a futile one.

One year later Clarkson showed up again, this time on the back patio of Salinger's house; Salinger was not surprised by his presence. The conversation was short, but Clarkson was able to ask the author why he never explained to his fans why he quit publishing. Salinger responded that publishing interfered with his private life and that he was not interested anymore in sharing his feelings with the public. Clarkson would go on to publish an article detailing the two encounters.[15] Was this the dealings of a manipulative reporter looking to advance his career by stalking an author who famously wanted nothing to do with him or men like him? Salinger certainly thought so. Ultimately, Clarkson was no more guilty of celebrity stalking than Salinger was when he sought out Joyce Maynard. One could argue that Clarkson's intentions were purer by far than Salinger's and caused much less damage. The private life Salinger so vehemently wanted to protect was far more troubling than misguided writers and fans seeking out their favorite writer because the man had hooked them and then cut them off. In the next decade, three men would also pursue famous people in the name of *The Catcher in the Rye*. Only they would not be seeking writing advice. They would be hell bent on murder.

Joyce Maynard, John Greenberg, Lacey Fosburgh, John Batchelor, and Michael Clarkson represented a public who simply refused to believe or accept that the author they loved and the work they adored was unavailable to them. These were people who risked the comfort of their lives, who dropped out of school, who broke the law, who risked their careers, for access to the author. Largely this emotional reaction befitting an addict stems from the emotional reading experience these people had when they read *The Catcher in the Rye* and the subsequent closet or prison to which Salinger retreated when he realized the effect his writing had on readers and the possible trail of bread crumbs that he was leaving that led to his sexual interest in young girls.

In the fall of 1978 the literary quarterly *New Letters* decided to reprint a story that first appeared in the magazine in 1940; it was a Salinger story titled "Go See Eddie," very likely the second piece of fiction he had ever published. Predictably, Salinger's agent at the time, Dorothy Olding, fired off a letter asking the magazine who it was that had granted them permission to reprint the story, causing editor David Ray to make the statement that he personally believed Salinger had abandoned his public. Ray had written the author multiple times over a five-year period and heard nothing. The story was documented in a 1979 *Chicago Tribune* article wherein Helen Dudar referred to Salinger as publishing's invisible man. Dudar started the article off by pointing out that Salinger was extraordinary in his refusal not only to make appearances or agree to interviews but to publish at all. What is a writer who does not publish or even try? Dudar reported that even at Salinger's publishing house Little, Brown, which still had rights to all his books in print, he was never accessible. Dudar related that generations of employees including publicists never even met the author and that it was clear among the staff that Salinger was never to be contacted for any reason whatsoever. According to Dudar, J. Randall Williams, who was a manager of the New York office but had since retired, had very little contact with the author— limited to the telephone and mail just in order to deal with the actual business of getting the books out. Williams himself related that Salinger was ridiculously particular about the smallest of details when it came to the books. For example, Williams believed that he sent out to Salinger at least twenty-seven different samples of white paper that would make up the jacket to the book *Franny and Zooey* before Salinger finally found one acceptable. In her article, Dudar also noted the many fans who seemed to regularly make pilgrimages to Salinger's Cornish, New Hampshire, home, convinced that Salinger would surely talk to him or her, mostly him. This seems ironic considering Salinger's own penchant for seeking out famous women whom he had only encountered on television, something that will be discussed at length in the next chapter. Dudar made an important point in her piece, that Salinger did not exactly guard his privacy as someone who merely wanted to guard one's privacy. He seemed scared. He once told a journalist in a rare telephone interview that publishing was an invasion of his privacy. *Publishing.* This was an exceedingly odd statement coming from a writer. Did *New Letters* force Salinger to write his short story "Go See Eddie" and submit it to their magazine? Did the magazine publish the story when Salinger was only twenty-one years old against his wishes? I contend that Salinger was fearful of what the work had to say about him and his sexual activities with young women. I think he knew the answers were in his work and he feared the next stranger who knocked on his door would be the police. [16]

"Go See Eddie" is an interesting story insofar as the primary theme of the story has to do with sex. The main character, Helen, is a part-time chorus girl and girlfriend of a married man named Phil who seems to be financing Helen's apartment where she can afford a maid named Elsie who may or may not be black. When Helen's brother Bobby shows up at her apartment, he implores her to go see Eddie about a chorus gig and laments that he has been hearing ugly rumors about her from some of his thug acquaintances in Chicago alleging that she has been hanging around with a different man from Chicago named Hanson Carpenter. Helen denies this accusation and claims that she and Phil have a real future together despite Phil already having a wife, a girl with whom Bobby has recently had lunch and apparently thinks is a classy woman. Whether Bobby actually had lunch with Phil's wife is unclear since Bobby clearly has motives of his own for urging his sister to go see Eddie about the chorus gig. Bobby continues to implore his sister to go see Eddie about the job, and Helen continues to reject the idea and hints that Eddie likely wishes to do more than just give her a job. Bobby then gets violent and knocks a hairbrush out of her hand and threatens to punch her in the face, the implication being that Bobby has somehow promised Eddie that he would send his sister over, perhaps as payment for a debt or as quid pro quo for a less than honorable favor. The story ends with Bobby leaving the apartment and again urging his sister to go see Eddie. After Bobby leaves, Helen calls up Phil and chews him out for allowing his wife to talk to Bobby and then calls up Hanson, seemingly to plan another date. Though Helen's sexuality is mostly assessed unfairly by her brother, who is interested in using her sex appeal for his own purposes, her own actions do suggest that she is dating a married man and carrying on with another man. This type of behavior would likely be respected were she a man, but since she is a woman she comes across as trashy. Helen may be the most sexual character in all of Salinger's oeuvre, including Sunny from *The Catcher in the Rye*.

In 2010 Ron Rosenbaum published an interesting article in *Slate Magazine* suggesting that "Go See Eddie" may represent a clue as to what Salinger had been writing after 1965. Rosenbaum cites Renata Adler's memoir *Gone* in which she mentioned that Salinger told her that he quit publishing because he wanted to write about sex. Based on this and Rosenbaum's discovery of "Go See Eddie," very likely in the magazine *New Letters* as a reprint from the 1940s that Salinger's agent tried to block, Rosenbaum speculates that Salinger's output since 1965 might be sexual in nature, even pornographic, that he quit publishing largely because he was writing about sex. Rosenbaum notes that in Adler's memoir she relates that Salinger told her that he was embarrassed to write about sex. The idea of Salinger writing porn is ludicrous, but what is interesting is that Rosenbaum seizes on what he considers a conspicuous lack of sex in Salinger's later work, as though the author was overtly trying not to be sexy. This would be in line with Salinger's fear that his own sexual behavior was codified in his work and would eventually come to light if he continued to publish good work that required total honesty. Or what is more likely, that Salinger quit publishing not so he could write about sex but so that he could be free to have sex with young girls. Rosenbaum several times references Seymour as an asexual, sexless character. This notion I find wildly inaccurate. In *Hapworth*, Salinger's last published work, the author presents Seymour as having a hyperactive libido as a seven-year-old boy who lusts after his camp counselor and makes an argument that his libido equals that of an adult, and that his siblings' libidos do as well. Salinger presents Seymour as the opposite of sexless, totally hypersexed to a fault on account of his age. Further, in "A Perfect Day for Bananafish," Seymour shoots himself after having what one could argue is a sexual encounter with a very young girl. [17]

The Attica prison uprising illustrated the potential effectiveness of protest as well as the intensity of fear and reprisal on the part of the state. This is what happens when interiority is revealed. Part of the logic that went into storming the prison and butchering everyone, including the guards, was that the state did not want the prisoners to set a precedent that could have been replicated across the United States. In other words, if the prisoners at Attica were successful, what would have prevented other prison populations from doing the same thing? This was the same sort of thinking that compelled the United States to get involved in Vietnam. In Vietnam, the threat was the spread of communism instead of the spread of human rights protests. When millions of people have a collective experience, impressive things are possible. This is what happens when fear compels people to hide their problems. Those problems tend to fester and then explode.

Nevertheless, there were positive outcomes from the Attica prison uprising. For one, after the uprising, public opinion began to sway in favor of prison reform. Secondly, the overwhelming focus of the demands of the prisoners at Attica centered on education, and this consequently had a profound effect on the possibility of education within prison. For Salinger, the 1970s was a decade of self-imprisonment plagued by fear of interior revelation that a public was rabid to draw out.

The interview Salinger granted Lacey Fosburgh in 1974 was his first interview in more than twenty years. The subject of the phone call had to do with the John Greenberg(s) hand-selling Salinger's uncollected short stories in two volumes. Among the stories in the two volumes were early versions of scenes that wound up in his only novel. Salinger was so bent on not publishing that in 1972 he returned his advance of $75,000 for his next book to Little, Brown. Salinger's decision not to publish at first glance seems like the act of a man with impeccable integrity. One additional reason Salinger refused to publish in the seventies was because he no longer had any financial need to do so. The fact that he could publish and did not fed an enlarged ego that was still deathly afraid of being compromised by any number of possible revelations the author wished to keep under wraps.

Attica's relationship to *The Catcher in the Rye* and the book's popularity in the 1970s centers on its fraudulent reputation as a novel of rebellion. When the true rebellion was going down inside the walls of Attica, where were the hundreds of thousands of readers who reveled in the popular novel of rebellion? *Catcher* had, in a sense, become associated with the sixties, a sort of idealistic attempt to change the world that was naïve and something to grow out of. Steinle notes,

> A college student in the 1960s . . . remembered that the countercultural slogan, "Don't trust anyone over 30" "seemed to come right out of Holden Caulfield's mouth," although as post-sixties disillusionment turned to apathy in the 1970s, [the student] necessarily "kept [his] distance from Holden Caulfield's identity crisis." Even so, [the student] acknowledged that when he would come across a copy of *Catcher* in a bookstore, Salinger's tale "always triggered memories of adolescence, of first discovering that I wasn't quite alone with my impure thoughts, that being an outsider wasn't all bad."[18]

That this man associated Holden's disdain for the establishment as part of the sixties counterculture is telling. Holden, like the Rolling Stones, is all talk. Consequently, once the man ostensibly grew up and put away childish things and presumably began working, he distanced himself from Holden's point of view. Another way of looking at it is that as a youth he sympathized with Holden's view but was not impelled to transform the trajectory of his political life. In this sense, the book is limited by its empty squabbling and its lack of any sort of fundamental engagement on the part of Holden.

The idea that *The Catcher in the Rye* is a book for kids may stem from the notion that the book is really about childish grousing with no adult political action to go along with it. Holden never really does anything about his complaints. He remains in the closet.

Salinger spent most of the seventies fighting off a segment of the reading public who refused to give up on the author. For the bulk of the readers who loved the book and whose tendencies toward rebellion peaked in the sixties, the seventies marked the return to the closet. The sobering result was a snuffed-out rebellion that could have used a generation of critical thinkers as allies in its struggle for basic human decency. William Kunstler represented a change agent, a catcher in the rye, who unlike Salinger at least attempted to come out of the closet, but it was too little too late, and even though there were some positive changes that occurred after and because of Attica, prison populations have exploded since, especially in America where two million out of the nine million prisoners worldwide are imprisoned, most of them folks of color.

5

CATCHER IN THE EIGHTIES

Lawsuits and Murder

For J. D. Salinger, the 1980s was a decade of litigation. When respected biographer Ian Hamilton, who had written a successful biography of American poet Robert Lowell, was commissioned by Random House to begin his dream project, a biography of Salinger, the author, who had spent the last two decades in the closet of his own making, was less than accommodating. For his book about Lowell, Hamilton relied a great deal on Lowell's letters. The biographer planned to use the same strategy for his book about Salinger. This was a mistake. The eighties also marked the first decade in which mainstream white crossover musicians like Vanilla Ice enjoyed commercial success by co-opting black culture *and* not only recognizing the appropriation but totally embracing it. The results were ambiguous, as the form of black culture musicians like Ice appropriated were largely based on stereotypes rather than any sort of progressive agenda that contested white supremacy. Further, the recognition and embrace did not obviate lawsuits on behalf of the black artists whose work was hijacked and sold. For the author of *The Catcher in the Rye*, the eighties was just another decade in which he failed to follow up on his promise as an artist willing to attack racial and sexual hierarchies like he did so marvelously in his only novel. In fact, the decade marked new heights the author was willing to go to ensure that he and his work remained in the white racial and sexual closet. The decade would also be remembered by fans of Salinger and his only novel as the decade of *The*

Catcher in the Rye assassins and would force the author to consider why three assassins cited his book as inspiration for murder. Indeed, the connection between Salinger and Mark David Chapman, John Hinckley Jr., and Robert Bardo stretch well beyond the novel.

Thirty-plus years of the hugely popular and controversial novel *The Catcher in the Rye* had rendered the book prone to academics on every level taking an intellectual swipe at it. Salinger's scant publishing record since the novel's release and subsequent notorious and celebrated hermitage had made him nearly as popular as the book itself and had made the book even more popular. The idea of a closeted political hero created by another closeted hero who one could not help but romanticize politically was too attractive for audiences and critics alike to pass up. In 1983 Ian Hamilton wrote to Salinger, telling him that he planned to write a biography of the author, assuring Salinger that he was a serious writer and was not to be confused with a mere fan. Salinger responded unequivocally that he was not interested one bit in answering any questions or aiding and abetting his own exploitation. In his response, Salinger falsely and perhaps wishfully suggested that it was possible for critics and fans to separate his life from his work. By dramatically ignoring the public, Salinger had ensured that readers would forever conflate his novel of rebellion with the reclusive author who lived in Cornish like a forested shaman.

His obsessive protection of his private letters from Hamilton on which much of his biography was based in particular captivated a reading public and further heroized the author and the narrator of his only novel. In the eyes of the public, the author was thumbing his nose at the man, sticking by his principles without having to do much of anything. What Salinger was an activist for was his right to do nothing.

In filing the lawsuit, Salinger made the letters public via the Library of Congress where anyone could go and look at them for a nominal fee. Salinger was banking on a slacker reading public who had sainted his closeted hero not taking the time. Shields and Salerno consider, "Why was he willing to take such a gamble? According to several of Salinger's ex-girlfriends we spoke with, one of Salinger's primary motivations was to prevent the exposure of his many epistolary relationships with very young girls—his pursuit, over many decades, of girls as young as fourteen."[1] Salinger feared that if these letters surfaced, scholars and the public would easily make the connection between his pursuit of these children and the most salient characteristic in his fiction, his use of children. Ironically, one year later in 1984 the *Chicago Tribune* released a one-page list of "25 'Must Read' Books for Students"; *The Catcher in the Rye* was ranked number eleven. *The Adventures of Huckleberry Finn* was number two, one spot ahead of the Bible.[2] This list was ironic since *The Catcher in the Rye* was evidently considered a must-read for students who were the very same age as children whom Salinger predated throughout his life.

Just three years later another legal fight having to do with cultural ownership and copyright law was brewing. As the legendary story goes, Death Row Records founder and former Los Angeles Rams replacement football player Suge Knight paid a visit to rap star Robert Matthew Van Winkle's (a.k.a. Vanilla Ice) fifteenth-floor Bel Age Beverly Hills hotel room to discuss Ice's hugely popular album *To the Extreme*. Knight's client, Mario Johnson (a.k.a. Chocolate), claimed that he had made major contributions to the album and deserved producer royalty points worth several million dollars. According to the legend, Knight showed up at the hotel room with six large men with guns, outnumbering Ice's armed and only slightly less meaty entourage. Knight's guys roughed up Ice's guys, and Knight took Ice out to the balcony for a pointed chat concerning the producer points. Here the story gets interesting. Again, according to legend, six two and 250-pound Knight dangled five eleven 165-pound Vanilla Ice over the railing of the fifteenth-floor hotel room by his ankles until he finally agreed to sign over the points. In later interviews, Ice denied that Suge hung him over the railing. Rather, Ice said, Suge told him to look down to the street fifteen stories below, the implication being that if he did not sign over the points he would be thrown off or might *accidentally* fall off the balcony. Either way, the threat was clear, according to Ice, so clear that he said he needed a diaper that night. Ice also denied that Chocolate ever made the major contributions he claimed to have made on the record even though the matter was later decided in court in favor of Knight and Chocolate.

The story of Robert Matthew Van Winkle's rise in the rap and hip-hop industry is instructive in that it illustrates the messiness and potential harm in racially crossing over without a political agenda. Ice's narrative is different from Elvis's and the Rolling Stones' in that Vanilla Ice desperately tried to cross over, knocking the door down with as much clamor as possible in order to be taken seriously in a genre that was decidedly black. The problem lay in Winkle's brand of blackness and the message it sent to white consumers about authentic blackness. Ice's motivation was not to challenge whiteness as a cultural construct but to rather capitalize on a musical genre that demanded one be well versed in cultural blackness.

While Salinger did not pay a visit to Hamilton and dangle him over a hotel railing, in 1987 the unwavering intensity with which Salinger lorded over the keys to his closet and refused to publish any work that might aid in cultural progressivism resulted in some bizarre legal arguments in relation to Hamilton's proposed biography. One argument Salinger's lawyers made was that First Amendment free speech rights also pertained to the right not to speak. In this case, Salinger's lawyers referred to their client's rights to not have his letters quoted in Hamilton's book, which constituted the heart of the book, a strategy Hamilton also used for his book about Robert Lowell. Another odd legal notion Salinger's lawyers invoked with respect to copyright law was that once a physical letter is mailed to a recipient the letter belongs to the recipient, but the content of the letter still belongs to the author of the letter. The United States Court of Appeals for the Second Circuit overturned the initial ruling, which found that the only injury Hamilton inflicted on the author was that of trespassing on his right to privacy. In the new ruling, Judge Jon O. Newman offered that what made Hamilton's book worth reading was the appropriation of Salinger's literary devices found in his unpublished letters, and since the letters were in fact unpublished though available in the Library of Congress, fair use did not apply. Further, the judgment suggested that their appearance in the biography might compromise the author's ability to profit from them when and if they were published at some point in the future. The result was that Ian Hamilton had to rewrite the book a third time, and in the third version the biography mostly detailed the difficulty and challenge of writing the book to begin with, which made for an interesting if somewhat unsatisfying read.

The publishing world took note of the extraordinary ruling, and along with Random House, the Association of American Publishers, and the Organization of American Historians, several authors appealed to the Supreme Court, but the case was ultimately rejected, thus upholding the previous ruling in favor of Salinger.[3] The publishing industry was highly interested in the ruling since most biographies of famous figures include some if not a lot of quoted material that falls under the fair use designation that protects the rights of scholars to quote brief excerpts of primary texts for the purpose of scholarship. While there is no doubt that the publishing industry after this ruling took great pains to ensure that biographers and scholars went through the proper channels for permission to directly quote from primary sources, the case itself could not be divorced from plaintiff Salinger, who everyone knew was not your ordinary, average author. In other words, Salinger's case was unique in that not all authors would be so obsessive about their letters being quoted in a biography. Many, if not most, authors would welcome a biographer writing a major biography about them. Would not that be evidence of one's importance? Salinger correctly feared that a biography would not wind up being about his greatness as a literary writer but rather about his less than noble personal life. It was not about being humble or rejecting egotism. It was about paranoia.

The final draft of Hamilton's book was described as nasty, vengeful, borne out of frustration, and vindictive, clearly not the adjectives Hamilton was looking for.[4] Once again, Salinger proved that he was willing to do almost anything to keep his private life private, even if that meant making a huge public stink about doing it. And once again, the reason Salinger was so ironically willing to sacrifice his privacy for his privacy was that he was actually only concerned about certain aspects of his privacy, namely, his sexual proclivities. Salinger had fully become white again, his single conscious monolith uncompromised by accusations of sexual misconduct, despite publishing one of the most antiestablishment, antiwhite culture novels of all time.

Rap and hip-hop was a genre of music created by black people and built with the discarded remains of late capitalism, virtual gold spun from a heap of broken technology and sound. Initially, rap and hip-hop represented a continuation of the black arts and black power movements, a platform on which to protest racial and economic inequities as well as the ongoing scourge in minority communities of police brutality. In this sense, rap and hip-hop were synonymous with the struggle for civil rights. Consequently, when rap and hip-hop proved to be commercially viable and later a booming business, blackness as an oppressed identity became the measure of its authenticity. The feeling was that authentic rap artists were from the hood, and because the hood was full of poverty and drugs and violence, these characteristics became defining ingredients in hip-hop culture and later black culture as a whole.

It is within this context that groups like the Beastie Boys and Vanilla Ice, white rappers and rap and hip-hop groups, came to embrace racial amalgamation. Unlike the Rolling Stones and Elvis, these groups embraced their black influences instead of muting them.

On the face of it, the Beastie Boys and Vanilla Ice might represent the kind of crossover race-changer that would have enriched the legacies of Elvis and the Rolling Stones in previous decades and saved the life of Meredith Hunter. After all, what Elvis and the Rolling Stones lacked was a sort of public racial reckoning and reconciliation with their black influences that included an active antiracist agenda. The problem is that the salient characteristics the Beastie Boys and Vanilla Ice used to mimic blackness became stereotypes that fueled racism.

These New York Jewish kids were not like Holden Caulfield railing against whiteness or the establishment. By the 1980s, anti-Semitism was very nearly invisible—though not extinct—and American Jews born multiple generations removed from the Holocaust enjoyed an existence free of the lingering dread present in the lives of their immediate forebears. The Beastie Boys had no political agenda with regard to their music. They merely copied what they considered authentic blackness and cashed in. Beastie Boy Adam Yauch (a.k.a. MCA) noted, "I kinda think of it like I think of the Rolling Stones playing the blues, stuff like that."[5] We can only take the Beasties at their word, that their foray into black cultural music carried with it zero political agenda, similar to the Rolling Stones. As was the case in the sixties, there was no shortage of political fronts in the eighties to get behind as drugs and violence threatened to swallow whole urban communities.

In short, not all crossing over is the same. For Elvis and the Stones, their crossing over was muted and in some cases denied and lacked any sort of political agenda that might have benefited the culture that they in effect robbed. For many of the white rappers who emerged in the 1980s, a decade of postmodern overlapping and synthesis, the melding of cultures resulted in the further negative stereotyping of black culture.

The impetus for white rappers to get into the hip-hop game was that hip-hop in the eighties appealed more and more to a white demographic that had plenty of money to buy records. Because rap was so heavily associated with a black experience imagined by a young white audience in relation to drugs, guns, sex, and violence, white rappers and eventually black rappers embraced these characteristics regardless of whether they had really lived through these experiences or grew up in the projects. In this context, Robert Van Winkle seized the day: "A tall white man with angular cheekbones . . . Ice superficially appeared to be recreating the Elvis Presley syndrome. . . . Vanilla Ice was trying to come across as a hardboiled gangster. . . . Few of his young fans cared where he grew up or what his ethnic preferences were. Maybe they wanted to act black themselves."[6] The brand of race-changer Vanilla Ice represented was not culturally progressive. He tried to reify his style of racial crossover based on inauthentic stereotypes he thought would sell. Ideally, a crossover artist or a race-changer would find a way to blend the best of multiple cultures and thereby create something that is not wholly one or the other but is positive in its combination. Or a progressive race-changer would challenge, indict, or complicate whiteness. What Vanilla Ice did was create a white version of a destructive stereotype that he felt signified black culture and validated his music.

For white suburban kids who imitate stereotypical blackness, the consequences may be real but are not irrevocable. They can enact a violent, thuggish persona and then take off their stereotypical blackness when they interview for a job. The blackness they sport is portable. For actual black people, whose skin becomes unfairly associated with the style suburban white kids into hip-hop adopt, they cannot take their blackness off when they interview for a job. And if that interview is with a white suburban dad who resents actual black people because his kid is wearing an oversized clock around his neck, the black applicant is behind the eight ball from jump street. It is this form of race-changer that black people resent. As was the case with Vanilla Ice, these suburban dabblers in multiculturalism had no interest in mixing with actual black people. To them, blackness was no more real than the eighties film *Colors*. In fact, to them, blackness *was* the film *Colors*.

This crossover equation is chilling. Adam Gopnik notes, "For a great many poor people in America, particularly poor black men, prison is a destination that braids through an ordinary life, much as high school and college do for rich white ones."[7] Gopnik further argues that as a result, a sort of U.S. prison exaggerated masculinity has quietly spread across the country across racial lines. White suburban kids mimicking a blackness that stems from commercial hip-hop and prison masculinity literally have no skin in the game. Consequently, their forays into cultural blackness become part of the problem instead of part of the solution to racial strife in the United States since the blackness they appropriate stems from the normalized mass incarceration of black people and the resultant hardened masculine style that permeates the country.

In the case of Vanilla Ice, "During the winter of 1989, [he] summoned the wrath of the hip hop community . . . by successfully marketing himself as a white rapper . . . [and] 'validating' his success with stories about his close ties to black poor neighborhoods. . . . Mr. Van Winkle [was] instead a middle-class kid from Dallas, Texas."[8] The strange but apt symbolism of Vanilla and Chocolate battling it out over black authenticity in rap music underscores the racial imaginary in which popular culture resides.

The success of Vanilla Ice and the Beastie Boys in crossing over and displaying a racial amalgamation composed of one part whiteness, two parts stereotypical blackness is that other black artists and moguls have bought into stereotypical blackness as a hot seller. As a result, there is a reductive split in the rap and hip-hop industry represented by gangsta rap (commercial) and conscious rap (political), with the former dominating the latter as well as the industry as a whole. To this day, gangsta rap has become synonymous with rap and hip-hop as well as black culture.

The story of Vanilla Ice's rise to popularity in the late eighties is the story of a crossover artist who aided in defining a culture by a reified stereotype. Despite the fact that Winkle was eventually forced to pay Chocolate for his contributions, the die was cast in relation to the damage done to the black community. These are the brands responsible for young black youth thinking that school is for white people and that reading is for white people. Racial crossover driven by commercial interests and unaccompanied by any sort of political agenda can have disastrous effects on the popular culture psyche. Alternatively, the reverse can be true, too. If crossover artists like Vanilla Ice can influence an entire industry and affect the way a culture is viewed, then a positive blending of cultures can have an equally powerful effect. Unfortunately, Holden Caulfield, Elvis, the Rolling Stones, and Vanilla Ice never attempted it.

For *The Catcher in the Rye*, the 1980s marked a break with any sort of monolithic reading of the novel. Like a reflection in a pond shattered by a rock, the novel would splinter and reassemble, its author emerging from his carapace if only to loudly exclaim his right to his shell. As Steinle notes, "By 1981 *Catcher* had the dubious distinction of being at once the most frequently censored book across the country and the second most frequently taught novel in the public schools."[9] High school teachers across the country thought highly enough of the book to risk being challenged by parents. On some level, it would appear that teachers wanted to be challenged, as though by teaching the book they were in some sense supporting a liberal and progressive cause. Nevertheless, this little hint of activism, anticipating the slacktivism of the computer age right around the corner, sated liberal educators who otherwise supported no active political agenda perhaps outside of the voting booth. Once again, Holden functioned as a mouthpiece for another generation essentially in the closet. Not only did one generation after another claim the novel as its own, but each generation claimed Holden Caulfield as itself. Holden represents the rebel in the closet, the slacktivist, the canary in the coal mine with no power to actually prevent the death of the coal miners. Holden is no one's catcher in the rye.

A new generation of critics began investigating the novel in the 1980s based on the postmodern theories that flourished in the 1970s. Despite the prevalence of these theories that often included questions of race, *Catcher* was never investigated in relation to racial themes.

Also in the 1980s, librarians who had been on the front lines of the censorship wars fought back. The American Library Association responded to the constant assaults on their titles by instituting "Banned Books Week" in September of 1982, to be cosponsored by the American Booksellers Association, the National Association of College Stores, the Association of American Publishers, and the American Society of Journalists and Authors, and endorsed by the Center for the Book of the Library of Congress.[10] During the week, books that had been targeted for censorship in the past were highlighted and prominently displayed in libraries. The program was so successful in its philosophy that censorship itself was far more dangerous than the targeted books that Banned Books Week continued and wound up being an annual event to open up the school year.

The decade of the eighties solidified Salinger as a closeted hero like his protagonist Holden Caulfield, ready and willing to fight tooth and nail anyone with the gall to take him on and expose him as anything less than fully white, including respected biographers like Ian Hamilton. To the reading public, both personages were characters who were highly admirable for their inaction. What Vanilla Ice illustrates is that the business of crossing over, of coming out of the closet as a race-changer, can be a messy business with disastrous effects when the crossover is not accompanied by an active political agenda that challenges whiteness. What Salinger in the 1980s further reminded us was that the author's inability to emerge as a true catcher in the rye was still informed by his shame.

Salinger's sixteen-year-old doppelgänger Holden Caulfield shares the author's complicated and at times misanthropic view of humanity. The smoldering bodies Salinger witnessed in the abandoned *Krankenlager* illustrated to him the potential depravity of human beings as well as the need for courage and love in the face of hate and injustice. The author imputed to his protagonist a simultaneous revilement and love for humans. This paradoxical relationship with other people caused the author to at times supplant regular human contact with the new and exciting medium of television, as well as movies, and eventually celebrity worship, traits also shared by his protagonist Holden and three American assassins whose lives at the time of their killings and attempted killing were deeply entwined with the novel. A predilection for seeking out human connection through television and film can lead to further alienation, low self-esteem, and resentment for the attractively contrived symmetry of dramatized lives. Like Holden does in the narrative, Salinger experienced hostility and feelings of inconsequence following his deep embrace of television, movies, and celebrity after he insulated himself in Cornish, New Hampshire. In both circumstances, as well as the narratives of three murderous devotees of the novel, the concomitant resentment following massive doses of the boob tube and silver screen along with celebrity apotheosis led to destructive fantasies and sometimes terrible violence.

Salinger's ambivalence about other human beings, particularly following the war, proved doubly difficult to negotiate since his vocation depended in large part on his ability to observe human life. As David Foster Wallace notes, "Television . . . [was] an absolute godsend for a human subspecies that [loved] to watch people but [hated] to be watched itself."[11] Television appeared to be a gift for misanthropic writers who required human observation but possessed a deep mistrust of human beings. This central paradox in Salinger explains not only his love of television and film but also his strange cat-and-mouse game with the media that marked the rest of his life. His all but complete rejection of real human interaction and embrace of dramatic lives and famous actors and actresses caused his own life to feel insignificant to the point where every now and again he felt compelled to remind the world that he existed and mattered and especially that unauthorized use of his work was forbidden. Further, it appears that he used his latent superstardom to seduce young actresses in addition to the young women he met on beaches and at parties.

Salinger emerged from the war leery of human beings and their capacity for violence and in search of an innocence exemplified in Oona O'Neil and his life before the war. Once he published *The Catcher in the Rye*, according to Jean Miller, the fourteen-year-old girl whom Salinger dated and seduced, he loathed all the attention both positive and negative.[12] While fiction writing is essentially a communicative act and assumes a readership, the communicative dynamic does not necessitate physical interaction between writer and reader. The process of fiction writing and reading allows an author one-sided communication and a reader one-sided consumption. Once fans of the book broke through this wall, Salinger acted as though a contract had been violated and by the third printing of the novel demanded that his author photo be removed.[13] Consequently, Salinger left the hustle and bustle of New York and the public eye for rural New Hampshire.

In 1953, Salinger purchased ninety acres of land in rural New Hampshire. The existing cottage he intended to inhabit lacked proper plumbing and a furnace. That first winter he pumped his own water for cooking and cleaning from a nearby stream and cut his own firewood for heat. Cornish, New Hampshire, represented a community that valued privacy, and though Salinger eventually did take part in local life by hanging out at a local juke joint and making his way to the local fair, his existence in the bucolic New Hampshire country was a far cry from New York high society. Not long after his move, he made friends with some local high school kids, even granting one young lady an interview for the school paper that wound up in the local paper, the *Daily Eagle*. As a consequence for the perceived betrayal, Salinger erected a wall around his home.

The gang of high school kids were mostly girls. The girls referred to him as Jerry and could always count on him to give them rides to the high school sporting events. They would all pile in his jeep and drive to the away games and afterward would often go to a restaurant. Jerry was part of the group. One girl assumed the boys did not accompany them because the girls and Jerry were too loud and the boys might get a headache. This reasoning sounds disingenuous at best. Likely the boys felt intimidated by the handsome man who had just published *The Catcher in the Rye* and realized that they could not compete with him for the girls' attentions and affections. One girl, Shirley Blaney, an aspiring writer and editor of the school newspaper and yearbook, began spending lots of time with the author and going on dates, likely without her parents' knowledge. She was blonde and beautiful and very popular and all the guys wanted to date her. When Shirley asked Salinger for an interview for the school newspaper, he gave it to her, but when he noticed that the story was not in the next issue he got suspicious and called up Shirley. She told him that the *Claremont Daily Eagle* had picked up the story, likely in exchange for money. In the story that Blaney wrote that came out in the local paper, Salinger was described as foreign looking, perhaps a comment on his Jewish ancestry, and was quoted as admitting that the character of Holden Caulfield was autobiographical. Also, and perhaps most upsetting to Salinger, was a somewhat random statistic Blaney offered, that 75 percent of Salinger's stories concern people under twenty-one years of age and 40 percent concern children younger than twelve. Salinger was furious and cut the high schoolers off after the story came out. Among the teenagers, the narrative was that Shirley wanted more than just a friendship with Jerry and betrayed him by making a fast buck by selling the interview to the local paper. The reality is much more sinister and obvious. A man in his midthirties had no business hanging out with and dating high school girls. When Shirley turned the tables on him and asserted a little control over the situation, Salinger immediately lost interest and hightailed it back to Cornish. At the beginning of the story, Blaney noted that Salinger was very good friends with all the high school students and then quickly added that he had many older friends, though, too. The story, in addition to displaying what Salinger surely felt was a betrayal and evidence of impurity on the part of Blaney, also exposed the author as a creep.

This was the last straw, or one of many straws, that turned Salinger further away from real people and drove him to that ersatz fountainhead of humanity, the television. It was no small coincidence that Salinger's foray into seclusion occurred simultaneously with the explosion of television as the dominant form of home entertainment. Throughout the decade of the fifties, the percentage of homes with television sets rose from just 9 percent to 87 percent.[14] By the end of the decade, the medium of television was the primary means by which American citizens connected with the world outside of their homes.

The sheer novelty of the medium prevented Salinger from realizing that large doses of cultural production could lead to the same kind of standardization of thought with which the Nazis inculcated much of Germany, or that much of cultural production demands an insidious conformity to the status quo. The kind of rigid acquiescence to and passive consumption of American culture that television demands can cause a sort of delusional emotional paralysis whereby the viewer at first feels as though he or she is a part of the culture portrayed on television and then sooner or later feels cut off and even jilted when television does not make good on its implicit promises of entitlement and happiness. Just like the Nazi façade of white supremacy promised power, prestige, and wealth while its foundation was built on exclusion, so, too, does television promise an existence only relatively few will achieve. Likewise, standardized capitalist culture as portrayed in American television culture emphasizes what one could have and could be but ultimately does not have and is not. Television legitimizes white entitlement and privilege by primarily depicting white people as the primary movers and shakers of American business, power, and culture. Consequently, when one's life does not mirror the fabulous white lives portrayed on television, television simply becomes a reminder of one's lack. Morris Dickstein explains the explosion of television in American culture in the 1950s:

> TV united the American public into a single audience even more than movies or radio had done, but it also privatized leisure time by relocating it in the home and focusing on family fare. . . . Highbrow critics saw only fragile kitchen-sink realism in live TV drama and little more than mind-numbing repetition in early sitcoms like *I Love Lucy* and *The Honeymooners*, which have been rerun ever since as classics of marital mayhem and anarchic social comedy. . . . Critics missed the crucial point that repetition and variation, not novelty, were staples of the popular arts. With its vast appetite for material, early television, like all popular media, relied on ingenious formula and the gusto of physical performance rather than the sort of originality that sustained high art. If the content of early TV was constrained by family values and conventional gender roles, there was a raw, ebullient energy that complemented the buzz and dynamism of American society.[15]

Two things are noteworthy here: one is that this form of entertainment occurred in the home instead of in public. While in the home can mean among one's family, it can also mean that the entertainment was consumed alone. Also, perhaps Salinger appreciated the commonness of television and perceived it contradistinctively to other forms of high art that he found pretentious and therefore despised.

By all accounts, Salinger made up for his limited exposure to actual humans by watching television and movies. Onetime live-in girlfriend Joyce Maynard, who was eighteen at the time, reported that Salinger could not get enough of television, especially Mary Tyler Moore and Andy Griffith, siphoning himself off from the world as he observed it through television.[16] Inherent in the idea of observing the world via television and movies is the illusion that television and movies accurately reflect human life, a misapprehension that often proves costly not only for the subject but also for the object of the fantasy. Prior to the advent of television, it is clear, according to Maynard, that Salinger was also an obsessive movie buff.[17]

Salinger passed on to Holden both his hostility toward people and his love for film. In the novel, Holden appears to use film as a sort of barometer for his relationships. How a person behaves in the theater or responds to a film signifies something important for Holden. One reason why Holden thinks so highly of his sister Phoebe revolves around her sophisticated filmic taste. Like Salinger, Holden seems to view the world through a movie lens as a result of his hostility toward actual humans.

The seeds for Salinger's ambivalence about Hollywood were sown long before he published *The Catcher in the Rye*. Before joining the army Salinger made clear his love for Oona O'Neill, daughter of perhaps the most famous American playwright who ever lived, Eugene O'Neill, only to find out not long after he joined that Oona had married Charlie Chaplin, perhaps the most famous movie star in the world. Not only was Salinger deprived of an opportunity to marry into a family that boasted an excellent and famous writer, but the man for whom Oona left him was himself an artistic genius in a medium that Salinger highly respected and at one time considered as a possible vocation. After Salinger joined the military, Oona left for Hollywood and hired an agent named Minna Wallis whose brother Hal Wallace was a high-profile producer at the time. As a result of her contacts and her vivaciousness, Oona quickly became a much coveted actress.[18] This experience perhaps more than any other ultimately caused Salinger to eventually resent the actors that largely made up his spectrum of human interaction. If he was not good enough for one actress and she left him for an actor, perhaps actors and actresses in general were out of his league.

While Salinger was a cadet at Valley Forge Military Academy, he was very involved in the theater.[19] Just before he met Oona, he considered acting or at least playwriting a viable career. At this point in his life, his identity was that of an actor. He was a member of the drama club at Valley Forge and played a role in every play that was produced in his two years there, often playing the role of women. His signature in his fellow cadets' yearbook was not his own but rather the characters' he had recently played. This was how he wanted everyone to remember him, as an actor.

Oona O'Neill was a socialite, a debutante who hung out at the Stork Club as a teenager and found herself photographed in the papers the following day sitting with movie stars and drinking milk. She was bright, sophisticated, and sexy. Salinger fell in love with her right away and found himself, if reluctantly, part of the New York social scene. In 1942, Oona was named debutante of the year. Oona's superficial fame upset Salinger, who once described her as "bright, pretty, and spoiled."[20]

Once Salinger joined the army, as far as he was concerned he and Oona were still an item and he wrote her letters every day. Then Oona simply stopped writing Salinger back, and pretty soon it was well known that she had married the most famous movie star in the world, Charlie Chaplin, and was in demand herself as an actress in Hollywood. Salinger wrote nasty letters to Oona, berating her for marrying a fifty-four-year-old man who was known to take monkey glands in order to perform sexually.[21] A famous actor had stolen his girl and made an actress of her.

That Salinger would criticize Oona for marrying a man much older in hindsight seems the worst sort of hypocritical indictment the author could possibly have made, but all that was still in the future for the jilted soldier. It is worth pointing out as well that when they were dating before the war Salinger was around twenty-two while Oona was only sixteen.

As Wallace notes, "Only a certain very rare species of person is fit to stand [the] gaze of millions. . . . The man who can stand the megagaze is a walking imago, a certain type of transcendent semihuman who, in Emerson's phrase, 'carries the holiday in his eye.'"[22] Salinger had a thing for those folks who carry the holiday in their eye, especially women, but watching so many movies and so much television reminded him of his first major heartbreak and reconfirmed that the beautiful women whom he constantly experienced as real people were too good for him.

Whenever he began to feel forgotten, ignored, dismissed, wronged, and inferior to the actors and dramatic situations he encountered on television, Salinger would contact the press to reinvigorate his sense of self. The result of Salinger both eschewing and courting the public by calling reporters and contacting famous women who were often television actresses was that his celebrity grew even more. What appears to be a hidden aspiration for fame, notoriety, and profit was driven in part by an insecurity stemming from too much exposure to television and movies and the actresses and actors who populated the medium.

His impulse to self-aggrandize suggests that he at times suffered from ignoring the public and relying on television and the movies for human contact. Salinger may have seen in his long battle with fame the same sort of suffering that served his art in the war. The next war for Salinger seems to have been his complicated relationship with celebrity. Similar to his gamble that the war would provide him with the type of experiences he needed to write meaningfully about human beings, he gambled that avoiding celebrity would do the same. In the case of the war, his gamble was correct; in the case of celebrity, he was dead wrong.

Like Salinger, Holden expresses a desire to run away from other human beings. Further, Holden, like Salinger, expresses a simultaneous infatuation and revulsion for movies, television, actors, and celebrity. On one hand, movies play an important role in his life, but on the other hand he loathes actors and is contemptuous of people who love movies. Along with Holden's disdain for movies is his particular disdain for actors and celebrity. Holden is jealous of the actors because they are often with gorgeous blondes. Holden tries to convince himself that he is just as good as movie actors and that he could get the girl, too, if only he deigned to want to act. Like Salinger, Holden loves movies but hates actors and one can only assume this idiosyncratic view stems from the same equation that haunted the author. Holden's hostility toward humans drives him to the movies, causing him to feel insignificant compared to all the people carrying the holiday in their eye.

Where Salinger responded to his bitterness and emotional insignificance by flirting with the press and writing letters to starlets and young girls whom he discovered in the newspaper, Holden's fear of other human beings and his subsequent obsession with movies causes him to feel as though his very existence is threatened. Like Salinger, Holden's constant obsession with movies and actors causes him to feel insignificant, like he is not good enough, as though his life is meaningless, and this manifests for Holden with a sense of literally disappearing in the middle of a city in broad daylight.

By all accounts, Salinger was prone to fits of fancy before he ever joined the army. His relationship with Oona O'Neill was the first indicator. Because his relationship with Oona never fully bloomed, it was easy for him to mistake the actresses and their characters for possible love interests or replacements for Oona. Elaine Joyce, a beautiful actress on the television show *Mr. Merlin*, received a letter from Salinger in 1981 detailing his admiration and suggesting a meeting. This would be Salinger's primary method of picking up women throughout his life. [23] Further, "In 1987 . . . Salinger fell in love with another television actress, Catherine Oxenberg, who was appearing on *Dynasty*. . . . Salinger fell in love with Oxenberg the moment he saw her on television. Salinger had an M.O. for television actresses. He would call them up on the phone and say, 'I'm J.D. Salinger and I wrote *The Catcher in the Rye*.'"[24] Salinger's early trauma with Oona along with his rejection of human interaction in favor of television and film and the concomitant diminished sense of self made him vulnerable to illusions built into heavy television viewing. He simply all but ignored the difference between the actresses and their characters.

Wallace notes:

> The people we espy on TV offer us familiarity, community. Intimate friendships. But we split what we see. The characters may be our "close friends," but the *performers* are beyond strangers: they're imagos, demigods, and they move in a different sphere. . . . This illusion is toxic. . . . Self-conscious people's oversensitivity to real humans tends to put us before the television and its one-way window in an attitude of relaxed and total reception, rapt. . . . The persons we young fiction writers and assorted shut-ins study, feel for, feel through most intently are, by virtue of a genius for feigned unself-consciousness, fit to stand people's gazes. And we, trying desperately to be nonchalant, perspire creepily on the subway. [25]

The illusion of an actual connection with the actors and actresses on television and in movies represents a chilling result of an overreliance on these mediums for human connection. The danger occurs when the dreamer ceases to realize or care that the dream is not real.

Mark David Chapman, John Hinckley, and Robert Bardo were all huge fans of *The Catcher in the Rye* who became obsessed with celebrities. In Hinckley's and Bardo's cases the celebrities were actresses. In all three cases, the result was fantasy and violence. These three individuals represent alienated men who like Salinger and Holden became obsessed with celebrity and lost touch with the real world. In all cases, the men were already alienated from society, supplanted normal human contact with celebrity obsession, and in the cases of the three killers, and arguably Holden, the separation or the collision with the illusion or dream resulted in violence. Playwright John Guare points out, "Chapman—who shot John Lennon said he did it because he wanted to draw the attention of the world to *The Catcher in the Rye* and the reading of that book would be his defense. And young Hinckley, the whiz kid who shot Reagan and his press secretary, said if you want my defense all you have to do is read *Catcher in the Rye*."[26] Lastly, Bardo brought along his copy of the book to murder the actress Rebecca Schaeffer.

Mark David Chapman grew up in Georgia and was a huge fan of the Beatles and rock and roll in general. Friends of his noted that he was in a rock band his freshman and sophomore years of high school but then underwent a significant change in his junior and senior years. The change described by friends and classmates had to do with a newfound religiosity. One friend described him as being very religious toward the end of high school, and another described him as a "Jesus freak."[27] Over the next eight years, Chapman worked as a printer and a security guard and developed an obsession with *The Catcher in the Rye* and John Lennon. At the time of the shooting of Lennon, Chapman was unemployed.

Mark David Chapman's evolution as a killer started with his sense of feeling like a nobody. Chapman was going downhill and becoming obsessed with John Lennon and telling his coworkers that he wanted to be Holden Caulfield. Chapman soon began to sour on Lennon and with Holden's influence began to accuse Lennon of being a phony and a sellout, a rich guy who cared little for his fans or for the music his fans loved and cherished or, more importantly, for the big ideas that populated his songs and developed into counterculture anthems. Like Salinger, Chapman's alienation resulted in celebrity worship that eventually resulted in further alienation and resentment. Just before murdering John Lennon on December 8, 1980, Chapman went to New York and traced the steps Holden took over the course of the novel, even hiring a prostitute. The morning of the murder Chapman had a copy of *The Catcher in the Rye* on his person, and right after he fired five rounds from a .38 outside his residence at the Dakota into John Lennon's back, Chapman sat down and began reading the novel.

According to reports, John Hinckley Jr. came from a respected white American family in an upper-class suburban community in Denver, Colorado. His older brother, Scott, was a popular athlete, and his sister, Diane, was a head cheerleader. John, on the other hand, due to his size and reminiscent of Holden, was the manager of his eighth-grade basketball team, and by high school had withdrawn from all extracurricular school activities and began playing the guitar. Hinckley attended Texas Tech for several years off and on, often skipping classes and taking impromptu road trips. Most of his credits were in history and many of his professors recalled that John was a good writer and particularly interested in German history and particularly Adolf Hitler and his book *Mein Kampf*. Hinckley joined the National Socialist Party of America, based in Chicago and founded to preserve the memory of Hitler's Third Reich. He was eventually kicked out of the group for being too extreme and promoting violence.[28]

The evening Lennon was shot, one of the mourners who congregated across the street was John Hinckley Jr., a man who was increasingly growing obsessed with the movie *Taxi Driver* and in particular the child prostitute in the film played by Jodie Foster. Hinckley had begun dressing like Travis Bickle. In the film, Travis Bickle harbors a violent hostility toward other people. Similar to Bickle's decision to enact violence to save Iris, "Hinckley settled on assassination as his best strategy to win Foster's heart, and on March 30, 1981, fired six times at President Ronald Reagan outside of the Hilton Hotel in Washington, DC. In Hinckley's hotel room, police found a John Lennon calendar and a paperback copy of *The Catcher in the Rye*."[29] The pattern here is the same. John Hinckley Jr., a failed songwriter who was prone to telling his family about fictitious girlfriends, became first alienated and then fixated on characters in movies. Robert De Niro's character especially appealed to Hinckley because he was also an alienated man who turned to violence to enact what he thought was a worthy and noble endeavor. Hinckley only became infatuated with Jodie Foster after he became infatuated with the film and the character Iris. In other words, Hinckley was not so much infatuated with Jodie Foster as he was with Iris, the character in the film. Like Salinger, Holden, and Chapman, eventually Hinckley drew no distinction between the performer and the real-life human being. And like Salinger, Holden, and Chapman, eventually this unsustainable collision of fantasy and reality led to hostility and violence. The impetus for violence was insecurity and feelings of insignificance. The impetus for Salinger's phone calls to actresses was to put himself on their level of celebrity, to prove over and over that he was good enough for Oona. Chapman felt justified in punishing John Lennon for what he felt was selling out. Hinckley felt that gunning down Ronald Reagan, perhaps not coincidentally another famous actor, would put him on an equal historic footing with Jodie Foster and therefore perhaps she would fall in love with him. Hinckley's white supremacy and Nazi sympathies reinforce the idea that his white upper-class entitlement fueled his frustration and resentment in relation to his feelings of insignificance. Why shouldn't he be able to win the love of a famous actress, or, more likely, Iris herself?

Robert Bardo was the son of a military man, and his family moved around a lot, finally settling in Tucson when Robert was thirteen. Within five years of living in Tucson, Bardo had developed an obsession with Rebecca Schaeffer, whom he only knew from his television set. The young man spent his time writing letters to the actress detailing his total devotion and love.[30] Soon Bardo could not take it anymore and decided to seek the actress out to prove his love and win her heart. Robert Bardo's infatuation with the actress Rebecca Schaeffer was also in part due to his feelings of insignificance that bubbled up while working at hamburger stands and going nowhere.

In 1989 Bardo began sending letters and postcards to the actress, extolling her as untarnished and unsullied by Hollywood. What Schaeffer did not know was that Bardo had already traveled to Hollywood a few times to meet her. After failing to make contact with her at Warner Bros. studios, where she was shooting the television show *My Sister Sam*, despite bearing chocolates and a teddy bear, Bardo paid a private investigator $250 to find out where she lived. Then on July 18, 1989, he showed up at her house and killed her. This time instead of a teddy bear, he brought along a copy of *The Catcher in the Rye*.[31]

Like Salinger and the three celebrity assassins, Holden goes from alienation to celebrity worship to fantasy to possible violence. Like the killers who experienced such a strong connection to the book, Holden enacts fantasies that sometimes include violence. Holden's alienation and hostility toward other people coupled with his obsession with movies facilitates fantasies that allow him to enact regenerative violence, violence that might perhaps render him as meaningful as the actors and actresses whom he resents.

There is an electric, galvanizing hostility coursing through the novel *The Catcher in the Rye*. Holden feels estranged from other human beings, alienated from normative discourse and relationships. Like Salinger, he seems heartbroken, depressed, and generally critical of women. Like Salinger, movies and television play a big role in Holden's life. He has clearly turned to these dramatic lives to get his fix of human connection, but these connections are illusory and only further his alienation. Salinger bequeathed to Holden his love of movies and his heartbrokenness and hostility toward actors and actresses that originated in his traumatic experience with Oona. As a result, both Salinger's and Holden's fascination with television and movies lead to further alienation and then fantasy, Salinger by falling in love with characters from television and trying to get their attention, as well as courting the press to prove his fame, and Holden by pretending he is acting himself and enacting violence on those around him who he thinks have wronged him and thereby not only gaining revenge but also transcending stardom. This equation clearly spoke to Chapman, Hinckley, and Bardo, men who also felt alienated, turned to the world of celebrity, became even more alienated and resentful, and eventually enacted fantasies and then violence that might have elevated their dreary lives. *The Catcher in the Rye* spoke to them as men who could not reconcile their feelings of emotional significance with their actual place in the world. These were all alienated men for whom television and the movies provided solace, even love, but it was an unsustainable love that resulted in anger, insignificance, and finally fantasy and violence when the object of their fantasies did not reciprocate that love, thus proving their phoniness. Salinger in this equation represents the progenitor, a man who turned to screen actresses because he could not stand to be around real people and also because his first real love was an actress. His first experiences with many of these women were through television while they were in character. His penchant for falling in love with these characters always stemmed from the heartbreak, insecurity, and humiliation of being bested by Charlie Chaplin. These were fantasies that Salinger was able to realize to some degree because of his fame. Holden, as an extension of the author, harbors the author's anxiety around real people, fascination with movies, and resentment of actresses, as well as his feelings of insignificance and inclination toward fantasy. In the cases of the three actual killers, Chapman, Hinckley, and Bardo, the fantasy is tinged with actual violence. The fantasy unrealized becomes the impetus for violence and death. For Holden, the violence is limited to fiction; for the three killers and their victims it was not. Chapman, Hinckley, and Bardo, along with being guilty of murder and attempted murder, were also guilty of misreading the novel. The alienation Salinger imputed to Holden stems from both Holden's closeted Jewishness and his indictment of exaggerated macho behavior that he attempts to articulate to the psychoanalyst driven in part by Salinger's own complicated relationship with masculinity based on the war, his physical deformity, and his relationships with young women. The feelings of alienation and inadequacy the killers felt were the result of unfulfilled white entitlement and white supremacy, an entitlement and racial hierarchy that drove Salinger to write one of the most banned books of all time. Salinger's predilection for indulgent fantasy relationships that redounded to Holden and manifested in his fantasy narratives of masculinity caused these killers to misread the novel as inspiration for their own masculine fantasy narratives and justification for ending the lives of "phony" stars who through their rejection proved their phoniness. Like Holden, who fantasizes about killing Maurice and winning the heart of Jane, a fantasy couched in the same exaggerated masculine terms that Holden attacks, the killers engaged in fantasies of their own in order to recoup their flagging sense of themselves as entitled white men that became all too real.

The eighties were a heady time for the author of *The Catcher in the Rye*. Seemingly everywhere he turned, people were hitching themselves to his novel to see whether it would pull them to stardom. Whether it was Ian Hamilton's attempt to write the biography of the century and thereby make a name for himself as the man who slew the famous reclusive and secretive author who had until then avoided anything nearing a biography, or the three assassins who felt justified in taking another human being's life in part because of what they found in the novel, Salinger had created a monster that he could no longer control.

6

CATCHER IN THE NINETIES TO THE PRESENT

Legacies

In the past quarter century, *The Catcher in the Rye* and J. D. Salinger have become, among other things, associated with mental health and artistic eccentricity. Movies have often portrayed lovers of the book as unhinged, maladjusted, or desperate to find the slippery author who before his death came to represent the elusive and mountainous wise man or shaman. Most of these cultural connotations were a result of the author's closeted existence against a world that arguably changed more in this span of time than it did since the turn of the century. Salinger's legacy of the closet in relation to race and sexuality provide an interesting lens through which to view two pre-Trump American presidencies beginning in 1992. On one hand, Bill Clinton has often been described as our first black president, a man whose modest upbringing and hip interests stereotypically resembled a nonwhite person's more than a white politician's. On the other hand, Barack Obama proved that no one had walked in his shoes. Both men, one could argue, operated within the confines of a closet and, like Salinger, failed to deliver the sort of leadership the nation needed.

The 1990s, according to some, brought about the first African American president of the United States, William Jefferson "Slick Willy" Clinton. President Bill Clinton was first elected in 1992 and first inaugurated in 1993. He would go on to win a second term and his presidency would span the decade. His often cited blackness apparently stemmed from his southern charm and affability, his modest if not troubled up-bringing, and his behavior in and out of the White House. Clinton's father died before he was born, and when he was a child his mother left him in the care of his grandparents, eventually returning and marrying a drunk-en, abusive man who became Clinton's stepfather. The blackest part of President Clinton's actions in the White House appear to be his sexual exploits, particularly with the intern Monica Lewinsky.

Bill and Hillary Clinton have always enjoyed strong support from African Americans. One might even conclude that Bill Clinton was the first high-profile race-changer who actually succeeded in melding aspects of both racial constructs, creating something new and better, unlike Elvis and the Rolling Stones. Or perhaps Bill Clinton has more in common with Robert Matthew Van Winkle (a.k.a. Vanilla Ice) in his unabashed desire to capitalize on racial codes in order to win over a demographic necessary for political success. If the cultural symbols that mark Clinton's blackness center on his alcoholic stepfather and his lurid affair with Mon-ica Lewinsky, then like Ice, Clinton simply advanced already entrenched stereotypes that fuel racism. If, on the other hand, his blackness pivots on his ability to overcome early challenges, his love for music, his southern dialect, and his easy way with people, then perhaps these markers really do offer us a blending, blurring, and unraveling of racial binaries. Clin-ton's ties to blackness run so deep that when our nation actually elected the first black president, Barack Obama, many argued that his blackness did not measure up to Clinton's.

That such luminaries as the great novelist Toni Morrison would refer to Clinton, even facetiously, as the first black president suggests that Clinton's blackness had some traction. Unlike Holden's blackness that stemmed from his author's Jewishness and experiences in World War II, particularly in relation to his contact with the victims in Nazi concentra-tion camps, Clinton's blackness was almost entirely symbolic, almost entirely since it is very likely that a DNA report would unearth traces of African roots as it would with almost everyone. Clinton's blackness was more in line with Elvis's, the Rolling Stones', and Vanilla Ice's, the product of cultural stereotypes and perhaps an affected style. On one hand, as with Vanilla Ice and commercial rap, black stereotypes can be terribly destructive for actual black people as they become reified and sold as authentic. Then again, some black stereotypes can promote solidarity and cultural belonging and awareness. The sort of transcendent race-changer whose experiences mark him or her as something other than white and who has the ability to build upon that experience and affect notions of race that might resonate for generations to come, similar to the opportunity Elvis had, is profound. Not only did the King have this opportunity but so, too, did the forty-second president of the United States.

Alas, Clinton's emerging blackness was politically expedient and his racial compromises in the 1990s worked in that they garnered him trust in the African American community. Coupled with the other attributes of his presidency, Clinton's badge of blackness now seems fraudulent. Only recently has his alignment with black people been called into question. The question is whether Bill Clinton earned the title first black president. He certainly could have. Did he emerge from his racial closet as a race-changer, or did he merely see an opportunity to capitalize on a black symbolic that came easily for him in order to garner a portion of the electorate necessary for his election? As Michael Dyson notes, "Clinton signed a crime bill that sparked a deadly spike in black incarceration and signed into legislation welfare reform that cruelly cut black bodies unable to find living-wage work from public assistance. . . . Clinton prefigured Obama's even more complicated use of black ideas and black identity while occupying the Oval Office."[1] In this view, Bill Clinton was far from the uncloseted race-changer that America needed in the 1990s. The power that he gained by mere gestures of crossing over demonstrated the potential in doing so. Ultimately, Clinton's blackness benefited him the most, and similar to the Rolling Stones and Meredith Hunter, just as Clinton was gaining power from his limited and closeted crossing over, thousands of actual black people were being incarcerated and cut off from desperately needed public assistance just when the decade could have really used a racially transcendent presidential figure.

Images of Rodney King getting pummeled by Los Angeles police officers in 1992 provoked a long-overdue national conversation about race and specifically police brutality. The beating broadcast all over the country promised a new racial consciousness that was now impossible to ignore. These images of a group of white police officers viciously beating a black man with their batons over and over again shifted the focus from the abstract to the concrete. No longer could anyone deny the existence of the type of brutality that had been going on for decades if not centuries. Overwhelmingly, Americans of all ethnicities sympathized with the man lying on the street being beaten and viewed the police officers as the criminals. The reverse positioning of good guys and bad guys shocked Americans' calcified assumptions about American justice. The subsequent acquittal of the men involved had the potential of sparking a national movement toward addressing police brutality and the inequities of a failed justice system. Instead, the protests and chaos that followed the acquittal of the police officers and in particular the violent encounter between Reginald Denny and angry protesters shifted the national consciousness from outrage at the acquittal of the police to disgust toward the protesters. The discussion transitioned from police brutality to rioting Californians.[2]

By the 1990s, *The Catcher in the Rye* had been beloved for more than forty years by adoring readers. What invariably occurred was that readers first read *The Catcher in the Rye* and were deeply moved by the book, which led them to other books by Salinger such as *Franny and Zooey*, which they also very likely loved, if slightly less so. Adoring readers then almost certainly moved on to *Nine Stories*, and for many perhaps their Salinger love affair ended. For hundreds of thousands if not millions more, *Raise High the Roof Beam, Carpenters and Seymour: An Introduction* came next, and if they were very resourceful and hungry for more Salinger they might have located *Hapworth* on microfilm or, much later, the Internet. For most, *Hapworth* was a disappointment and did not quench the thirst of a public hankering for a reading experience like the one they had in *Catcher*. This unrequited romance almost certainly led Salinger fans to wonder why their favorite author wanted nothing to do with them and seemingly had no interest in satisfying their hunger for more characters like Holden Caulfield. The result was that by the 1990s Salinger was as famous, if not more, for his reclusivity and failure to pacify a reading public for nearly a half a century as he was for writing one of the most beloved and feared books of all time. Consequently, fans looked to the man himself, viewing his body as the only text that continued to tell the stories they wanted to hear. In the nineties, *Catcher* was the tenth most challenged book[3] and in 2002 Holden Caulfield was chosen as the second best literary character of all time, behind only Jay Gatsby from F. Scott Fitzgerald's novel *The Great Gatsby*.[4] In short, the old fights and forces were still very much at play and the novel was as popular and feared as ever.

This is why events like Salinger's house catching fire in 1992 became big national news. Shields and Salerno note, "This was the first time—in 1992—that the public learned of Salinger's third wife, forty years his junior. Colleen, a nursing student who worked as an au pair for someone else and married in the early 1980s, met Salinger, corresponded with him, and left her husband for the author."[5] Once again, the salient information one gains from this is that while Salinger was in his sixties he was busy seducing a woman in her early twenties with the same last name as the one woman who started it all—O'Neill—and while certainly not illegal, this revealing fact still strikes one as a little strange and perhaps worth hiding since it pointed to past transgressions involving far younger women the author had been paranoid about for most of his life.

After four decades, Salinger's legacy had solidified and petrified into a cultural joke that fed into the mystique and myth of tortured genius. When word got out that Salinger's novella *Hapworth 16, 1924* that first appeared in the *New Yorker* in the sixties was going to be released as a book in 1997, *Saturday Night Live* parodied the news by reporting that Salinger's only comment about the long-awaited release of the novella in book form was, "Get the hell off my lawn."[6] Like most of the breaking news in relation to Salinger since the sixties, much of the attention centered on Salinger himself and his notorious reclusiveness. The reports about *Hapworth* focused on a small publishing house in Virginia named Orchises Press. It was perhaps not surprising that the idiosyncratic author chose a small house instead of a large one since it never seemed like his goal was to actually sell books or build a large readership. Rather, it was as if the author wanted just the opposite: the fewer readers the better. When word did get out, there was an explosion of critical activity in relation to the novella and almost all of it bad. One review in particular by Michiko Kakutani in the *New York Times* was especially scathing. Kakutani, who would receive the Pulitzer Prize the following year for her body of trenchant criticism, hammered everything in the story, from its characterization and plot to its petulant tone and total lack of charm.[7] She accused the author of poking holes in Seymour's saintliness in order to pander to critics who slammed the character's one-dimensionality. Likely, Kakutani was alluding to Seymour's prepubescent sexuality, which had nothing to do with the novella's critical response and everything to do with Salinger himself. The review did not help the prospects of the book being published.

Ultimately, the book was never released in book form. Eventually the owner of Orchises Press, Roger Lathbury, took the blame, saying that he had arranged the book's publishing and even met with the author in a restaurant but leaked the deal prematurely. Lathbury wrongly assumed Salinger wanted to actually sell books, when very likely the impetus for the publication was Salinger's desire to have full control of the book, which at that point he did not have since it had originally appeared in the *New Yorker*. The publicity the book received before it was even published was at odds with Salinger's reasons for publishing it in the first place.

The 2000s brought about 9/11, the election of our first black president not named Bill Clinton, and the death of Salinger. In addition to George W. Bush's cowboy presidency functioning as a gateway to a black intellectual making it all the way to the White House, 9/11 also played a role in that for a time Middle Easterners and particularly Muslims became the new black people. Actual African Americans, as have Jews, at least for a short period of time, benefited from the extreme hatred and racism aimed at Muslims and Middle Easterners, which, in part, led to Barack Obama's presidency. Alas, this was short lived as Obama's presidency quickly caused the original sin to come bubbling forth in earnest and with a venomous passion.

Obama's presidency demonstrated that crossing over and race-changing is a messy and difficult process. In some ways, Obama was victimized by the one-drop rule: one drop of whiteness making one automatically *white* instead of the other way around. There is no term for a black person acting too white, though the sentiment certainly exists. Perhaps that is because for a long time the goal of many black people was to lighten the race. Within the logic of colorism, the whiter the better, and if one can actually pass, then more power to him or her. Therefore no pejorative term developed in relation to a black person being too white. And yet, Obama's presidential legacy has been marred by white racism and black indictments of Obama's whiteness or lack of blackness.

Obama's presidency inspired "[posters] of Obama dressed as an African witch doctor, online images of First Lady Michelle Obama depicted as a monkey, and racist Facebook comments by white people. . . . [Americans] have come to a grim conclusion: *I didn't know how racist America was until it elected its first black president.*"[8] The level of racism aimed at Obama called into question the first black president moniker bestowed on Bill Clinton, and yet Obama was often compared unfavorably to Clinton as possessing an inferior blackness. Oftentimes this accusation was leveled at Obama by other black people. These statements pulled double if not triple duty in that they indicted Obama for not being black enough, which implied that he did not do enough for black people, but they also signified a blackness based in part on sexual prowess, a destructive stereotype partly responsible for Clinton's dubbing as the first black president, and singularly responsible for perpetuating the myth of the black rapist, a myth responsible for perhaps hundreds of thousands of killings of black men over hundreds of years. After Reconstruction, freed slaves no longer possessed value as slave labor and so their lives were more vulnerable after slavery. In order to undo the gains of Reconstruction, black men were murdered in vast numbers. As justification for their murders, which often involved lynching, black men were painted as beastly rapists hell bent on raping white women. The sexualization of black men as justification for their murder continues to this day. The comment also worked as an example of the dozens, a game of put-downs popular in black culture. Attacking Obama's blackness by suggesting that he lacked sexual prowess hearkens back to the homophobia and hyperbolic masculinity associated with the black power movement, an association often cited as the reason for the movement's limitations. This indictment alluded to the kind of blackness that people expected from Obama, a blackness that ultimately had little to do with skin color, a blackness that was rooted in a political agenda that resulted in real legislation that helped black people. The dark side of this indictment alluded to a brand of black masculinity rooted in homophobia.

What is at stake in Obama's presidential legacy is the idea that his mere presence in the Oval Office signaled that America had achieved racial equality and that no more programs or rhetoric with regard to race was or is necessary. By virtue of a black man being president anyone can be president. It certainly proved that black people no longer had an excuse as to why they lagged behind in many statistical categories. This was and is obviously not the case.

The question then remains: How can a nation elect a black president and still have racial problems? Or better yet: How can a nation elect a black president and then become racially more intolerant? One answer to this question is that Obama purposely did not address race in any sort of sustained way because he did not want to be thought of as simply a black president with a black constituency. He wished to be regarded as a regular president with the whole United States as his constituency, most of which were not black. In other words, the charge is that in order to get elected, Obama had to mute his blackness. This would suggest that he merely viewed himself as a symbolically transcendent figure instead of a revolutionary one.

Because of Obama's reluctance to come out of the closet as a black man for fear of the country pigeonholing him as a black man, he was vulnerable to charges of whiteness. Early on, Obama's biracial upbringing caused some critics to wonder if he really was black and what he really would be willing to do for black people. Questions regarding Obama's blackness underscored the idea that blackness exists irrespective of skin color. Blackness in this sense is necessarily wed with political action. Therefore not only could an African immigrant who voluntarily came to the United States not be black but an African American could not be as well.

What exactly are we talking about anyway when we refer to someone's blackness? It appears as though one's skin pigment is only secondary to one's political agenda and cultural positioning. Consequently, one's actions become the measure of one's blackness, as opposed to one's skin color. Skin color, then, becomes irrelevant and merely symbolic of power structures. Whiteness does not denote white skin; rather, it denotes who is in power.

The problem with Obama's closeted blackness was that it allowed black people to remain in the closet as well lest they upset the apple cart. This is not to say that Obama remained in the closet completely. He certainly peeked out from behind the curtain at times to remind a devoted electorate of his blackness. The problem was that his effortless embrace of black culture did not necessarily translate into change for black Americans.

Some might argue that the Obama presidency was a zero-sum game. The benefit of a black presidency perhaps does not outweigh the false notion that America is finally enjoying a postracial society, especially when the black presidency adopted a sort of Jackie Robinson style of presidency, taking it on the cheek and not fighting back for fear of perpetuating entrenched stereotypes and ruining it for others who would inevitably follow. One wonders, though, what might have occurred if Obama had emerged from his racial closet on day one. Perhaps he would not have won a second term, but perhaps the conversation about race would be different.

In 2009, Salinger found out that a sequel to *The Catcher in the Rye* was being planned for publication and release later that year. The news appeared in a British newspaper and quickly spread to American papers. The book, titled *60 Years Later: Coming through the Rye*, was being released by Swedish publisher Fredrik Colting through Nicotext, an imprint of Windupbird Publishing whose catalog included joke books and porn. Later reports confirmed that in fact Colting wrote the book himself. Purportedly, the book focused on Holden Caulfield as a seventy-six-year-old man wandering the streets of New York after busting out of his retirement home. [9]

Predictably, Salinger's legal team, including his longtime agent at Ober Associates, Phyllis Westberg, found the book grossly derivative and totally reliant on the original. In the "sequel" Holden suffers from incontinence, and Phoebe has become a drug addict. In Colting's text, Holden seeks out Salinger in Cornish because the author has revived the character in order to kill him. At issue was whether Salinger owned the character Holden Caulfield. As the legal fight developed, Colting's side clung to the idea that their book was a parody of the original and transformative enough to be considered an independent work. At ninety, Salinger was not about to be present for any sort of deposition and so Westberg acted as a stand-in for the author and freely offered that the writer was now totally deaf and recovering from breaking his hip. News about the legal battle, rather than exciting the reading public about Colting's book, fanned the flames of Salinger and *Catcher* fandom. The only legible Salinger artifact that was not static in time, the man himself, was breaking down. Newspaper editorials and the Internet exploded with love letters and narratives from fans about their first encounters with the beloved novel and their subsequent lifelong relationship with it. It had been a long time since anyone had heard from Salinger, and news about the author's mortality struck a pathos among his fans that hovered between wistfulness, love, and frustration. The courts eventually ruled that Colting's sequel was derivative rather than parodic or transformative and banned it from the United States. Part of the decision noted that despite the fact that no authoritative picture of Holden Caulfield existed, his image was thoroughly recognizable and consequently copyrightable. [10] The argument suggested that everyone knew Holden despite never actually seeing him embodied. He was indelibly etched within the collective mind of the cultural psyche.

Philip Marchand of the *National Post* wrote an article about the legal battle and drew an irresistible comparison between Salinger and Michael Jackson. The article actually spent very little time on Colting's book and quickly digressed to the legacy of Salinger. Marchand argued that Salinger's legacy was really about the strain of growing up, referring to this as the grudge against adulthood. Marchand characterized both Jackson and Salinger as man-children and referenced Jackson's Oprah Winfrey interview where he said he enjoyed tucking in young boys at night when they slept over at his compound Neverland. This admission became sinister and tragic when several boys accused Jackson of sexual abuse. The comparisons between Jackson and Salinger are rather obvious: their refusal to grow up, fixation on children, and charges of sexual abuse, as well as their living in a compound where they attempted to create a fantasyland beyond the eyes of a public who adored them and made them rich and famous. Marchand went on to make perhaps an even more arresting point when he touched on the racial aspect of Jackson and the historical trope of the white man-child and his nonwhite male counterpart, evident in classic American novels like *The Adventures of Huckleberry Finn* and *Moby-Dick*. In these tropes, the nonwhite counterpart allows the man-child to indulge his impulse toward adult negation since the nonwhite counterpart is disqualified from American manhood anyway. Marchand noted that Salinger had no equivalent, and that Jackson tried very hard to be the white figure in the black/white equation. I would argue so did Salinger. Like Jackson, Salinger did his best to ultimately prove his whiteness, and his nonwhite counterparts were mostly young girls.[11] Other interesting comparisons that one might draw in relation to Salinger and his fame and fixation on youth would perhaps be Woody Allen, who often wrote about older male protagonists having relationships with very young women in, for example, the film *Manhattan*, where a forty-two-year-old man dates a seventeen-year-old girl. When Allen was well into his fifties, his then-partner of over a decade, Mia Farrow, discovered that he had been having an affair with her teenage adopted daughter Soon-Yi Previn, whom Farrow had adopted when Soon-Yi was five years old. Allen would later be accused by Farrow and others of sexually abusing their daughter, Dylan. In all these cases, the writing was on the wall, so to speak. It is just that no one was paying attention.

On January 27, 2010, Salinger died. As Shields and Salerno note, "In keeping with his lifelong, uncompromising desire to protect and defend his privacy, there [was] no service, and the family [asked] that people's respect for him, his work, and his privacy be extended to them, individually and collectively. . . . Salinger had remarked that he was in this world but not of it."[12] The problem for Salinger and for his most famous protagonist and the millions who read the book and identified with the character was precisely that Salinger and Holden were in this world but not of it. Salinger created a character who lambasted a culture that he essentially did not have the courage to change. It would appear that the motivating factor behind his closeted persona was the sexual closet in which the author resided. He extended this closet to Holden with the added layer of race. Not surprisingly, many of the obituaries that notified the world of the author's death drew attention way more to his reclusiveness than to his enduring work. In a *Washington Post* article, the title read "After Catcher in the Rye, Writer Became Famous Recluse" and in the *International Herald Tribune* the title read "J. D. Salinger, Reclusive American Author, 91; Obituary." The *Washington Post* article, in addition to quoting *The Catcher in the Rye* and suggesting that reading it has come to represent a rite of passage for adolescents, quickly delved into the life of the author and his vehement rejection of the reading public. Bart Barnes interestingly broached Salinger's relationship with Joyce Maynard and noted that sex between the two was not great, the implication being that because of this Salinger dismissed her. This is interesting since Maynard maintains that intercourse did not happen. Barnes also offered up Sylvia Welter as an unequivocal Nazi, a fact that is unsubstantiated but likely. Finally, Barnes pointed out that in Salinger's daughter Margaret Salinger's memoir *Dream Catcher*, Margaret (or Peggy, as she was known) laments that her dad preferred the characters in his fiction over his own children and had very little contact except with pen pals until he actually met them in person. One cannot help but wonder who these pen pals were and surmise that they were mostly the Joyce Maynards of the world, young, impressionable women often in troubled families looking for a catcher in the rye.[13] In the *Herald Tribune* piece, Charles McGrath suggested right off the bat that Salinger was famous for not wanting to be famous and also referenced Maynard later in the piece.[14]

The takeaway from these two obituaries is that the most salient aspect of Salinger by the end of his life was not the work that made him famous and remained the purest part of his existence, something he ostensibly was after, but rather his compulsion to abscond with young women to his remote hideout and the obsession with keeping this a secret. Perhaps the greatest irony of Salinger's life was that the purest thing that he created was the very thing that drove him from the public. If the narrative about his life is correct, that what he was after once the war was over was something pure, he had it in his writing, especially *The Catcher in the Rye*, and in trying to protect its purity and himself he sullied the very thing that actually was pure and good, so much so that by the end of his life he himself was the brighter star, not the work.

That *Catcher* is a beloved book is not surprising; neither is it surprising that it is also a much feared book. The book demonstrates the closet but also the door. Despite all this, by the time of Salinger's death, his legacy was cemented.

In 2013 David Shields and Shane Salerno released the film and accompanying book *Salinger*. The two together provided Salinger fans and scholars an exhaustive portrait of the man and his work. In their work, Salinger's penchant for young girls and the devastating effects of World War II, in particular his experiences liberating the Nazi concentration camps, came to the fore. The two also confirmed the rumors that over the years Salinger indeed had been writing, and writing a lot. They note:

> Based on private interviews conducted over nine years, we have learned that J. D. Salinger approved works for publication. . . . The first book is titled *The Family Glass*; it collects all the existing stories about the Glass family together with five new stories. . . . Salinger has also written a "manual" of Vedanta—with short stories, almost fables, woven into the text. . . . In addition, there is one novel, a World War II love story based on Salinger's complex relationship with his first wife, Sylvia Welter. . . . Salinger has also written a novella that takes the form of a counterintelligence agent's diary entries during World War II, culminating in the holocaust. . . . Separate from the new Glass stories, the Vedanta manual, and Salinger's new war fiction is a complete retooling of Salinger's unpublished twelve-page 1942 story "The Last and Best of the Peter Pans" . . . one of the earliest of the Caulfield stories, in which a very young child nears the edge of a cliff. This reimagined version of the story will be collected with the other six Caulfield stories as well as new stories and *The Catcher in the Rye*, creating a complete history of the Caulfield family. [15]

Shields and Salerno note in *Salinger* that these books were to begin to appear in 2015 and then be rolled out over a five-year period ending in 2020. At the time of this writing in 2017, no books have appeared. One wonders whether Salinger changed his mind from the grave, still unsure whether he was giving away too much in these works, whether someone would show up at his door to arrest him. What is clear is that if and when these books are released, critics will be able to further measure their arguments up against more original work from the author.

Also in 2013, perhaps in part as a way to ride the wave of revitalized interest in Salinger due to Shields and Salerno's documentary and book, especially since it does highlight Salinger's sexual proclivities, Joyce Maynard, the bright-eyed eighteen-old-girl who left Yale to come live with the author after he had read an article of hers and written her a letter, published a sort of bitingly ironic article in the *New York Times* titled "Was Salinger Too Pure for This World?" In the article, Maynard claimed that more than a dozen women had contacted her over the years since she had published her experiences with the writer who was almost thirty-five years older that she, one of which was a teenage girl with whom he was in contact while living with Maynard. Maynard revealed that the letters Salinger wrote her were unmistakably in the voice of Holden Caulfield and that she found this voice irresistible. She said that she thought at the time that she would be with Jerry forever. She was eighteen. A year or so later, Maynard said, Salinger gave her two fifty-dollar bills and sent her away. Maynard also noted that there was an unwritten and unsaid rule that any communication with the man was to be kept a secret and if that rule was broken, then it was proof of one's impurity. The most important point that Maynard made in her article was that over the years Salinger's work has been for the most part exempt from serious critical scrutiny ostensibly due to the works themselves being so beloved by the very critics who might look critically at them. Maynard's point and perhaps call was for critics to take a look at Salinger's work in light of the new revelations in Shields and Salerno's documentary, that Salinger did in fact carry on these affairs with very young women. Maynard lamented the fact that recently critics have still been giving Salinger a free pass, essentially shrugging their shoulders to the new information. Maynard cited one fourteen-year-old girl that she communicated with who described Salinger in godlike terms and told her that Salinger broke off the relationship once they had sex. This was likely

Jean Miller. Maynard maintained that these relationships were consensual but questioned the ethics and morality of people in positions of power using that power to instigate emotional and sexual relationships, something Salinger most certainly was guilty of. Maynard confessed that at one point Salinger told her that she was worthless and always would be. She said that any man who would tell her that, now that she was fifty-nine, would not last long in her presence or in her mind, but when she was eighteen Salinger's words had a devastating effect, not only since she had aspirations of being a writer like Salinger but also in relation to the simple indignity of being treated so poorly. Maynard noted that the documentary *Salinger* seems to claim that Salinger's interest in very young women was an attempt to reclaim innocence that was lost in the war. What she said is absent from the film is a consideration for the innocence that he took in the process of trying to reclaim his own. [16]

Backlash to Maynard's tell-all book about her relationship with Salinger and her subsequent choice to sell his letters to her was nothing new. In 1998, Howard Kissel reviewed her book *At Home in the World* for the *New York Daily News*, titling his piece "No Cause for Re-Joyceing Maynard Looks Back, Yet Again—This Time at Her Life and Some Time with J. D. Salinger," which in and of itself hinted at a sort of tired act on the part of Maynard of self-promotion. In the review, Kissel accused Maynard of the habit of naïve writing, since her first piece was an autobiography at eighteen years of age titled "An Eighteen Year Old Looks Back on Life," the very article Salinger read and on the basis of which contacted the young girl and eventually convinced her to drop out of Yale and come live with him in Cornish, New Hampshire. Kissel also drew attention to Maynard's virginity at the time of her relationship with Salinger, pointing out that she refused to have sex with the author but regretfully found other ways to please him, which had the effect of not only sexualizing her but also implying that she was a tease. Finally, he capitalized on her admission that the article she wrote and published in the *New York Times* at eighteen was in part fiction, by asserting that her book about Salinger may also be made up. [17]

An even more egregious response to Maynard was a piece that came out in the *Washington Post* in 1999 written by Jonathan Yardley called "Lecher in the Rye? Hardly." In this article Yardley referred to Maynard as an exploitive predator for her decision to auction off Salinger's letters. Yardley's basic argument was that even though Salinger may have had ulterior motives for contacting her when she was eighteen, two wrongs do not make a right and her turn in the realm of benefits was not justified. He argued that at eighteen Maynard's reasons for responding to the author and eventually dropping out of school to live with him were as ignoble as the author's motives. This was wildly offensive and ignorant and placed the blame on the young women who find themselves manipulated into relationships with powerful older men, oftentimes through intimidation and implied threats. Yardley viewed Maynard's relationship with Salinger, who was almost thirty-five years her senior, as wrought with selfishness from the start. Yardley's point was patently ridiculous and offensively apologetic for older men who prey on vulnerable women, especially when they are in the same industry and the older men are successful. Clearly Yardley was not aware that Salinger had been doing this his whole life.[18]

Films such as *Conspiracy Theory* (1997) and *The Good Girl* (2002) have employed *The Catcher in the Rye* to establish a character's personality, exploiting the novel's association with instability and rebelliousness, but in 2015 Samuel Goldwyn Films, almost unbelievably the same film company that butchered "Uncle Wiggily in Connecticut" in its film *My Foolish Heart*, released a movie called *Coming through the Rye*, written and directed by James Steven Sadwith, that relies on the novel for the entire narrative of the film. In *Coming through the Rye*, a sixteen-year-old boy named Jamie decides to adapt the novel into a play for his senior thesis as a way to thumb his nose at his oppressive boarding school and its students whom he finds dense and phony. His English teacher forces him to acquire Salinger's permission in order to produce the play, and most of the film centers on Jamie's quest to locate the author for that purpose. Like Holden, Jamie is a Jew in a WASPy boarding school trying to cope with his brother's death and deal with his sexuality. Along the way, Jamie meets Deedee, a sexually aggressive sixteen-year-old girl who agrees to drive Jamie to find Salinger and attempts to have sex with him along the way in a hotel room. Jamie refuses for reasons that are unclear, underscoring a strong homosexual undercurrent in the film that culminates in Jamie admitting that he loves another boy toward the end of the film. Despite this admission that Jamie qualifies by strangely saying that he is not interested in kissing this boy, the film's treatment of sex and sexuality is awkward and clumsy and offers little insight into Jamie's motivations or realizations.

Jamie eventually does locate Salinger, who is played by Chris Cooper. Cooper's portrayal of Salinger suffers from a flatness of characterization overly reliant on Salinger's fame as a crotchety loner hell bent on being left alone. The film demonstrates how Salinger's refusal to publish and disavowal of the reading public obscures any message the novel or the film may or may not possess. In the end, whatever message anyone wishes to derive from the novel or the film is obscured by Salinger's flamboyant hermitry. The sexual awakening of Jamie and Deedee never happens and never really makes any sense in the film because the connection is never made between Salinger and his sexual history, including his interest in very young girls and likely abuse at the hands of adult men. Salinger's habit of using kids in his work stemmed not from wanting to protect them but rather from wanting to have sex with them, likely a result of his own tragic experiences of sexual abuse as a child.

In early 2015, Anisa George's play *Holden* debuted at the New Ohio Theatre and ran again in January 2017. Set in Salinger's writing bunker in Cornish, New Hampshire, the play involves a cast of characters, including Salinger himself, that in part represent the cultural American space the novel inhabits and its odd story as it has taken on a life of its own in spite of the author. The main characters in the play, along with Salinger, are Mark David Chapman and John Hinckley Jr., as well as a twenty-something man named Zev. Ostensibly Chapman and Hinckley are present in order to convince Salinger to publish again, and they feel like it is their fault that he quit since he might feel to blame for the violence they enacted in the name of his only novel. Several times in the play Chapman in particular says that he feels it is his cosmic duty to help Salinger publish again. On the surface, this is Hinckley's purpose as well. Zev's role in the film is unclear at first but later emerges as the link between Chapman and Hinckley and contemporary mass murderers who one reviewer described as radical losers, or young men who fall through the cracks of late capitalism and take it out on humanity via mass shootings.[19] The only other character in the play is Salinger's daughter Peggy, who makes a few brief appearances and in addition to humanizing Salinger at the end of the play inadvertently comments on the temporal structure of the play via the children's book that she is reading called *A Wrinkle in Time*. The plot revolves around whether Salinger will actually finish the book that he is currently working on. One can see chapters of the manuscript hanging from a clothesline in the bunker. Eventually Salinger does finish the book but then dramatically places it in the safe along with the other manuscripts that he has finished but never published over the years, something Chapman and Hinckley are trying to prevent him from doing. The other plot strand is in relation to finding out who the other characters are in the bunker and what their relationship is to the author. Hinckley we find out about right away, but we don't realize Chapman is Chapman until later in the play. The emotional center of the plot revolves around Zev, whose relationship with the author is murky at the outset. Eventually we realize that Zev is interested in breaking the record for mass killings and that he is in the bunker as a symbol of contemporary male violence linked with the author, Chapman, and Hinckley. Zev admits that he was forced to read *The Catcher in the Rye* in high school but did not think much of it. He, unlike Hinckley and Chapman, does not cite the novel as inspiration for his violent tendencies, which has the effect of absolving Salinger in the long run as the lone cause of Chapman and Hinckley's violent acts, since Zev's violent desires highlight that a man's actions are ultimately his own. Zev's tenuous connection to the novel and the author allows him to escape the bunker, leaving Chapman and Hinckley, who cannot escape or do not want to since their identities have over the years become of a piece with Salinger and *The Catcher in the Rye*.

George's intriguing play involves nearly all the subtexts of the cultural history of the novel and the author. For example, Salinger's experiences in the war play a front and center role in the play. Both Chapman and Hinckley wear some form of army fatigues, Chapman's pants and Hinckley's coat, and Salinger's army helmet is a significant prop when Zev puts it on and asks Hinckley to hit him on the head, which Hinckley does repeatedly and with enthusiasm. The piece of fiction that Salinger is working on is about the liberation of the concentration camps, likely the very book Shields and Salerno reference in *Salinger* that allegedly consists of diary entries by a counterintelligence officer leading up to the liberation of the camps. Salinger's character has very few lines in the play, but at one point laments that the liberation of the camps was not a liberation at all and mentions all the bodies stacked up like wood. The stacks of wood that make up the walls of the bunker allude to the bodies Salinger found when he entered the *Krankenlager* and to which he adds throughout the play, the implication being that Salinger and his work have possibly in some way contributed to the death toll. In the play, Salinger clearly suffers from PTSD and when lying on his cot endures terrible nightmares stemming from his war experiences. At times the atmosphere literally transforms into that of war as bombs and explosive flashes illuminate the shadowy bunker. Several times Chapman and Hinckley appear wounded and morph into figments of Salinger's dreams, indicating that the bunker is really a mental space of Salinger's made up of the war and the cultural impact of his novel, especially in relation to Chapman and Hinckley, who killed or tried to kill in its name. George also broaches Salinger's own role as death dealer when Zev wonders how many people Salinger might have killed in the war and whether his actions were any different from Hinckley's and Chapman's. When Chapman says war is noble, Zev and Salinger laugh at him. In this sense, George underscores a link of violence among all the characters and highlights the significance of the war vis-à-vis Salinger and *The Catcher in the Rye*.

George injects racial themes into Salinger's bunker in the form of Zev, a barely veiled white supremacist who finds Anders Breivik's mass killing in Norway inspiring. On July 22, 2011, in Oslo, Norway, right-wing extremist Anders Breivik detonated a bomb, killing eight people, and then nearly two hours later and twenty miles away dressed as a police officer boarded a ferry to the island of Utøya in Tyrifjorden and indiscriminately killed sixty-nine people, including victims as young as fourteen. Breivik self-identified as a national socialist and railed against a tendency toward multiculturalism that he viewed as Europe's cultural suicide driven by feminism and Marxism. Zev's enthusiasm and admiration of Breivik mark him as a white supremacist, similar to Hinckley who was a noted Hitler enthusiast. As Chapman lists all of Salinger's forays into various religions and alternative healing practices, his Jewishness comes up. Zev gets in Salinger's face and claims that he is a phony Jew in a very menacing way, evincing his barely veiled hostility toward difference of any kind.

Sexuality also plays a role in the play in the form of homoeroticism. At one point, Hinckley and Zev wrestle, and as Zev dominates Hinckley he seems to turn Hinckley around and pelvically thrust at him several times as though fucking him. At times Chapman gets in bed with Salinger and snuggles up with him in his cot. Salinger also dances romantically with Hinckley. Further, Chapman's seemingly out of the blue conversation about two female swans that get mistaken for a male and a female alludes to the ducks in *The Catcher in the Rye* but also to nonnormative sexualities, androgyny, and infertility or laying eggs that never have a chance to hatch and become actual swans, arguably a metaphor for Salinger's writing after 1965.

The allusions and symbols of nonnormative sexualities undergird the play but never really emerge as a coherent motif. Certainly in the novel Holden is preoccupied with sexuality and at times worries whether he is gay. He also encounters several gay men, including Luce, Antolini, and the cross-dresser who may or may not be gay at all. This preoccupation was driven by Salinger's own sexual insecurities likely stemming from his predilection for very young girls and missing testicle. This aspect of his life comes to the fore by way of his daughter Peggy, who exists as a stand-in for all the children who populate Salinger's work, including Phoebe and Holden and also unfortunately the young girls Salinger sought out his whole life as sexual partners. Just as *Catcher* ends with a young girl, so, too, does the play as Peggy seeks out her father in the middle of the night after having a nightmare, providing the sense of innocence and purity that Salinger is seemingly after. Peggy also very importantly delineates the time-space structure of the play by alluding to a wrinkle in time or time travel, the idea of being able to access different places in time without changing the present, which is similar to the wrinkle of time in which the play exists, as at no point were all these characters the age they are in the play at the same time.

Anisa George's play *Holden* is important because she manages to encapsulate all the major themes of the Salinger machine in a coherent narrative. While the play exists in a space that can be attributed to Salinger's own mind, it also exists in a kind of collective cultural space that in part has been the creation of not only Salinger but a reading public who has given narrative to the novel in spite of its author.[20]

Yet another film about Salinger and *The Catcher in the Rye* called *Rebel in the Rye* premiered at the Sundance Film Festival in January of 2017 and was picked up by IFC Films and scheduled for a wide release in the fall of 2017. According to advanced reviews, the film covers Salinger's early life in New York and his attempts to publish his stories, his relationship with Oona O'Neill, his war experiences and subsequent mental breakdown, and the publication of *Catcher* and the resultant rejection by the author of fame and notoriety. Many of the reviews point out that the film fails to deal with Salinger's relationships with young women and tries to romanticize the writing life and myth of tortured genius. In short, the reviews suggest that the film is not very good. In Guy Lodge's *Variety* review, he refers to *Rebel in the Rye* as Hollywood's retaliation for Salinger not allowing *The Catcher in the Rye* to be adapted. Lodge goes on to describe the film as clichéd and phony. Lodge makes it a point to note that the film takes zero risks and glosses over anything in the writer's life that may alter the standard view held by adoring fans.[21] Jordan Hoffman's review of the film in the *Guardian* all but dismisses the film as shallow and only mildly interesting and suggests that it wouldn't have been a crime had the film never been made.[22] In the *Hollywood Reporter*, John DeFore describes the film as trite and mentions that it nearly goes out of its way to overlook Salinger's relationship with very young girls.[23] Looked at in combination, these reviews describe a film that in no way deviates from the narrative of a man who went to war, wrote a book, and nobly shied away from the attention. This sort of insight into Salinger ignores everything that is actually interesting about the writer and what humanizes him and makes him ultimately worth reading.

That two major films and an off-Broadway play have emerged in the last two years evidences that Salinger and *The Catcher in the Rye* have not been this relevant to the culture since the novel was first published. This is likely the result of David Shields and Shane Salerno's documentary and book that came out in 2013. It has simply taken this long for writers and artists to digest all the new information. Salinger might also simply represent the last interesting American writer.

Salinger's death occurred at a time when race in the United States was at a point of critical mass. Obama's presidency forced Americans to confront an actual black man in a position of power on a daily basis. No longer was it easy to control the cultural production of the black image. This caused many Americans to make a choice, be it internally or externally, about how to respond to Obama as their president. Many could no longer contain their boiling racism and joined racist movements like the barely veiled tea party, while others found the courage to exit their racial closets and embrace their country and its first black president. The legacy of Salinger and *The Catcher in the Rye* rather than centering on the book's antiestablishment antiwhite message evolved into a comment about mental health and artistic genius. Salinger's most interesting text proved to be the man himself. That in the last four years there has been so much productivity in relation to the author and especially his only novel demonstrates that Salinger's legacy as a man and a writer has yet to fully play out. What are all these writers, including myself, grappling with? What is the draw? Certainly one reason for all the activity has to do with Shields and Salerno's biography and the promise of more Salinger work. Sometimes it takes decades for a writer's legacy to crystallize. For example, Ernest Hemingway nearly became absent from reading lists in college American literature courses since he was roundly dismissed as a hypermasculine white writer, part of a group of dead white men who had made up a literary canon in dire need of reevaluation. But then as more criticism appeared attesting to his masculine insecurities and odd relationship toward sex, driven in part by his posthumous works such as *Garden of Eden* and his classic novels like *The Sun Also Rises* that featured an impotent protagonist struggling with his masculinity, all of a sudden Hemingway emerged as once again worthy of further critical inquiry. Likewise Salinger's story has not ended either.

CONCLUSION

As a Ph.D. candidate at the University of South Florida, I was assigned to teach an Intro to Literature course to mostly sophomores and decided to use my all-time favorite novels as primary texts, including *The Catcher in the Rye*. It had been many years since I had read the book and I was happy to find that it still held up well and offered a rich tapestry of events and subtexts for undergrads to analyze. My overall response to the novel had not changed a lot from when I first read it as a teenager except that this time around my focus was on guiding students through their own analyses. I had never personally written about the book, largely because I never really found an argumentative angle that truly interested me. While I still regarded the book as seminal in my journey as a critical thinker and writer, I perhaps unconsciously associated it with my youth and did not consider it in relation to my publishing and career goals. In other words, I did not think writing about *The Catcher in the Rye* was going to get me a job.

That all changed in 2013 when I watched David Shields and Shane Salerno's documentary *Salinger* and read the treasure trove of material that composed the accompanying book. Some of the information that Shields and Salerno offered in the documentary was already available in biographies but not nearly with the same detail or scope or corroborated by so many close to Salinger. The jaw-dropping news for me was realizing that Salinger was Jewish and that he was one of the first soldiers to liberate the concentration camps after World War II. This changed my whole view of the book. Now there was a reason Holden hated white bourgeois culture. Now there was a reason he was sympathetic to the marginalized. It took a near breakdown on the part of the author to create a character against whom the confederacy of dunces conspired.

The book Salerno and his partner Shields released to accompany the documentary, chock full of interviews and raw material, fell short of a cohesive text but contained a gold mine of data for enterprising scholars. Several of the interviews highlighted the degree to which Salinger was insecure about his masculinity and sexuality. Shields and Salerno documented several instances indicating that Salinger was wildly insecure about his missing testicle and his penchant for very young girls. They quote Salinger as complaining that due to his "ailment," he would be marked as unfit for regular military duty with the rest of the "faggets [sic]."[1] Further, several interviews implied or outright argued that Salinger's reclusiveness was due to his desire to keep his long history of pursuing young girls under wraps.

Together these items of information allowed me to construct a nexus between author and protagonist and an overall argument that illuminated Holden's internal conflict as well as make sense of the author and novel during the decades after it was published. According to interviews, Salinger never denied that Holden was a stand-in for himself. Once that was established, I felt confident in conflating the two to some degree. I could argue that Holden's internal conflict is driven by his sympathy for the vulnerable, stemming from Salinger's experiences in the concentration camps and his alienation as a Jew in a WASP-controlled world. Further, I felt confident in arguing that Salinger's fears of emasculation or sexual persecution prevented him and Holden from fully coming out of the closet as true race-changers or catchers in the rye for marginalized people and ultimately drove his silence after the last of his published work appeared in the midsixties. If the explosion of interest in Salinger and *The Catcher in the Rye* in the last two years, including a major play and two major films, is any indication, there were many others like me who had the same eye-opening experience when watching *Salinger* and reading the book that went along with it.

Armed with a completely new reading of the novel, I decided to teach it again and found many college students open to reading Holden's criticisms in relation to a dominant white culture from which he feels alienated. One student responded after reading the novel that "honestly, it seems like white people are reserved for his scorn more than any other race, possibly because it is his own race. In the same way that he holds himself as the example that other people aspire to, he almost seems to think his own race is being stupid for embracing what he thinks is phony."[2] Another student noted, "I honestly couldn't find any overt or implied references to race, though that simply could be because I am missing something. I tried to look online for instances that I may have passed over, but I couldn't find anything."[3]

I was also interested to see how high school students around Holden's age in the book might respond to the novel in 2015–2016. I was able to organize a book club at a local high school and pick the brains of some high school students. When I asked students whether Holden seems like a typical rich white kid, one student responded, "I feel that Holden is not like a typical rich white kid. My reasoning for this is the fact that he dislikes phonies. . . . As a result, Holden becomes an outlier from the 'typical rich white kid' stereotype. I think that if he did do the things a typical rich white kid would do, then Holden's mindset would be completely different."[4] Another high schooler wrote, "No, because he's more complex than your stereotypical rich, white kid. He's very intelligent and sensitive, but he suffers from mental paranoia and stress."[5] Another student very astutely answered my question about whether Holden seemed like a typical rich white kid by writing the following:

> Yes, I think so. In the beginning, we are meant to think that Holden is different than all the phonies at his school. However . . . I came to the realization that Holden is just as fake as everybody else of his status. He lies to get what he wants and often acts only to benefit himself. Holden doesn't even realize how privileged he is—he tosses around money like it's nothing and doesn't care that he was given the opportunity for an education that most people don't have access to. Deep down, Holden has some good traits, but that doesn't excuse the way he acts.[6]

The responses I received from both college and high school students reinforced my sense that Holden's disdain is primarily reserved for the dominant white culture in which he feels vulnerable but that he is unwilling or unable to fully disavow.

Whiteness, like traditional American masculinity, draws its power from members who define themselves contradistinctively to other groups. Michael Kimmel notes, "Such a list of 'hyphenated' Americans—Italian-,

Jewish-, Irish-, African-, Native-, Asian-, gay—composes the majority of American men. So manhood is only possible for a distinct minority, and the definition has been constructed to prevent the others from achieving it."[7] While Italian, Irish, and Jewish American men have for the most part assimilated into the ranks of normative masculinity, African American, Native American, Asian American, and especially gay American men still for the most part remain excluded. For American masculinity and whiteness, maintaining the hierarchical power structures necessary for these divisions requires marginalizing or othering particular groups. One might view whiteness as the dominant racial construct that fraudulently claims a monolithic status and then defines others as different and therefore inferior. Steve Martinot points out that

> "race" names a system of socio-political relations in which whites define themselves with respect to others they define as "nonwhite" for that purpose. Because whites are the definers, "race" is inseparable from white supremacy. That is, "race" as a concept is inseparable from the white hierarchical domination that constructs it.[8]

In many cases, whiteness is invisible to its members. Born into a system of privilege, one unknowingly enjoys that privilege without even recognizing it. For example, Salinger may not have fully confronted his racial borderland as American Jew and probationary white man until he witnessed the atrocities at the *Krankenlager*. Holden's tenuous whiteness is at the forefront of his interior attacks of white culture. Martinot further notes, "Whites are not born white. There is no inherency to being white. They are given their whiteness by the white supremacist society into which they are born."[9] In light of this statement, one can view Holden's internal conflict as his struggle to reject or embrace a whiteness that he knows is destructive.

The one novel most associated with *The Catcher in the Rye* is Mark Twain's *The Adventures of Huckleberry Finn*. Huck Finn's voice was based on a young black boy whom Twain encountered on his comedy circuit. That Huck's voice is the voice of a black child complicates the racial history of American literature since it is often said that American modern literature began with the voice of Huck Finn.

Salinger's and Holden's reluctance and inability to emerge as true change agents in life and in the novel can be likened to a person hiding in a metaphorical closet. Salinger represents the most reclusive and closeted

American writer in history, the last interesting American writer. What he seemed to be hiding was his sexual preference for very young girls and possibly his testicular deformity that he equated with manhood. Holden shares the author's sexual masculine insecurity with the added layer of his closeted Jewishness. The novel presents a character who enthusiastically voices his dissatisfaction with American culture but does nothing about it. This sort of closeted grousing spoke to generation after generation as a viable response to a culture marred by inequality and police brutality. The book signifies the liberal political mind-set that privileges empty activism. Consequently, decade after decade legislators have been elected into office who do not represent the will of the people.

The latest presidential election galvanized a voting bloc to come out of the closet and fill the void that the liberal majority had left. As Jennifer Agiesta notes, "The biggest story of the 2016 election is undoubtedly the rise of Donald Trump, and behind the Republican nominee is a group in its last throes as the biggest force in politics: The white working class."[10] Trump's emergence as the Republican nominee for the president of the United States and subsequent election depended on the last gasp of a demographic hostile toward ethnic inclusivity and multiculturalism. The secret these closeted whites had prior to emerging from their closet was their immense and powerful feelings of white nationalism and feelings of disempowerment as the electorate moved beyond white supremacy toward an embrace of diversity. As more and more people of color engaged in the political process, dominant white society became less powerful. As a result, a particular group of mostly white males, sometimes referred to as working-class whites, or uneducated whites, have answered Trump's clarion call to make America great again by supporting the prospect of rounding up Mexicans, banning Muslims, and reinstituting stop and frisk in major cities. Trump's demagoguery and racial dog whistles amazingly caused this group who represent the most privileged in our culture to present themselves as left out and marginalized. Their unified push for Trump has demonstrated the power in coming out of the closet as a politically active force.

Obama's eight years in office reflected an electorate no longer anchored and driven by white men. Consequently many white men feel as though the government has alienated them:

84% [of working-class whites] say their views are not well represented by the government in Washington, well above the share of white college graduates or black or Hispanic working class. . . . About 6 in 10 white working class people say it's gotten harder for people like them to get ahead financially and two-thirds say it's harder to find good jobs. Many are concerned about what the next generation will face: 50% say they expect their children to have a lower standard of living than they currently have.[11]

These numbers reflect the lamentation of a group used to privilege and white supremacy but who can no longer expect to count on it. These folks realize their children will actually have to compete with other American ethnicities on a more equal playing field. They realize for the first time in American history that whites without college degrees will not make up the largest voting bloc of the American electorate. Not surprisingly, the number one concern of this group is nonwhites. More than any other group, they believe that "immigrants today are a burden on the United States and that the government should attempt to deport all immigrants currently living in the US illegally."[12] This group is for any activity that reinstitutes white supremacy, whether that means deporting millions of immigrants, banning Muslims, adopting stop and frisk in major cities, or disempowering women. When only half of the American electorate votes in any given election, any energized voting bloc can have a tremendous effect on an election.

The impetus for Holden's book-long diatribe against Pencey Prep and aggressive macho men like Stradlater and Maurice stems from the tremendous effect the Holocaust had on J. D. Salinger. That he wrote *The Catcher in the Rye* in foxholes and on the side of the road while involved in some of the deadliest battles of all time cannot be underscored enough, nor can the fact that he wrote the second half of the book after witnessing the horrific cruelty that had been visited upon primarily Jewish inmates in the *Krankenlager*. Salinger's Jewishness had a profound effect on his view of the United States. All these qualities are apparent in Holden Caulfield as he spends much of the book attacking various U.S. cultural power structures and hierarchies with a particular disdain toward aggressiveness and macho white male culture.

Salinger's experiences in World War II impelled a sympathy toward marginalized and vulnerable identities that he imparted to his protagonist Holden, who for much of the novel worries about Jane Gallagher and whether she was raped by Stradlater and her stepfather. Throughout the novel, Holden displays sympathy for women, cross-dressers, homosexuals, and the ducks in Central Park. His dream of becoming a catcher in the rye stems from his empathy for these vulnerable beings. Holden ultimately fails to be anyone's savior since he cannot relinquish his investment in the very male macho culture that he derides. Throughout the novel, he engages in the very macho, sexually aggressive, and homophobic behavior that he laments, relegating his criticisms to a sort of interior closet that only reveals itself to the shrink with whom he is sharing his story and the reader who is indirectly privy to his thoughts. Holden's reluctance to come out of the closet regarding his sympathy for alternative sexualities and his distaste for macho culture mirrors Salinger's own closet that he famously inhabited for most of his adult life. Salinger's penchant for privacy may have involved his testicular deformity that plagued him and caused him much insecurity as well as his sexual preference for very young women that he attempted to hide his entire life but that drove much of his work. Holden's internal conflict in relation to masculinity is shared by Salinger. On one hand, the author was very aware of the disastrous effects of hypermasculinity and the concomitant superiority of self-described Aryan white men. What Salinger evidently failed to realize was that sexism and the sexual manipulation of young women were of a piece with white supremacy. Controlling and subjugating white women has long been crucial in maintaining the fraudulent idea of Caucasian blood purity. Salinger's less than honorable, less than innocent, and less than pure pursuit of teenage girls is at odds with the ideology of antiwhite supremacy at play in his great novel *The Catcher in the Rye*.

The narrative that takes place through the decades in relation to the novel reflects the narrative within the novel. Holden's penchant for critical thinking without action appealed to youth who were fatigued by their parents' stuffiness and intense desire to conform, mostly driven by the fear of spreading communism and witch hunts of difference. This energy peaked in the sixties and petered out in the seventies with only modest cultural gains mostly due to the efforts of marginalized American groups and women. By the end of the seventies, white readers considered Holden a wonderful reminder of their wild and exciting but naïve selves in the sixties. It was time to grow up by the eighties.

Along with all the various ways that Holden exists within a closet, including his Jewishness, his sympathy for marginalized sexualities, and his distaste for macho culture, are his feelings of desperate alienation, his love of movies, and his violent masculine fantasies. This equation was mirrored not only by the author of the text but also by three men who cited the novel as inspiration for murder: Mark David Chapman, John Hinckley Jr., and Robert Bardo.

J. D. Salinger's first love, Oona O'Neill, may be responsible for Salinger's penchant for young women that continued throughout his life. His harrowing experiences in the war coupled with the disaster that was his relationship with Oona O'Neill drove him from other human beings. As a consequence, he resorted to the exploding medium of television to keep his eye on human life, something that is critical for an author. This reliance on television coupled with his emotional need to re-create his relationship with Oona compelled him to seek out famous actresses whom he first encountered as characters on television, a sort of willful ignorance of the chasm between fantasy and reality that may have been driven by the sublimated resentment of Oona O'Neill and all actresses to whom Salinger may have felt inferior.

Holden also displays a disdain for humans and a conflicted fascination with the dramatic lives on-screen. He is at once very interested in films and at the same time terribly insecure and critical of famous people. He also enacts masculine fantasies that are often couched in violence. This equation of alienation, fascination with television and movies, and fantasy and violence were mirrored in the three assassins who cited the book as inspiration. Mark David Chapman, John Hinckley Jr., and Robert John Bardo all turned to aggression and violence toward famous people as a result of feelings of alienation and white entitlement. All three of these men felt lost and insignificant in their lives and saw something in *Catcher* that spoke to them as alienated white men who resented famous people, especially women. These men could not reconcile their meager existences with their identities as privileged white men and saw in Holden a model for rising above it, namely, through acts of self-righteousness and violence. Whether it was killing John Lennon or Rebecca Schaeffer or attempting to kill Ronald Reagan, all these men took their cue from Holden, who enacts violent fantasies as a response to his alienation informed by the author's own masculine insecurities and obsession with actresses.

I have chosen to view the decades since the publication of Salinger's *The Catcher in the Rye* through the lens of decade-defining events and men who, like Holden Caulfield, failed to relinquish their whiteness in favor of a better world. These men, like Holden, had opportunities to do so, were in some ways compelled to do so, were in positions to do so, but ultimately failed to do so, or were, as with William Kunstler, too late in doing so.

Holden Caulfield confesses his interiority to another human being who has the legal obligation to keep it confidential. He does not act. This slacktivism ultimately appealed to a large swath of the public who exorcised their distaste for an oppressive culture not by activism but by grousing and then by doing nothing but accepting the dominant fiction of white male privilege. Eventually this led to the explosion of social media and psychotherapeutic drugs, ways of coping with a disappointing and out of control culture. Now everyone is a Holden Caulfield online and Donald Trump is the president of the United States.

I did not set out in this book to sententiously criticize Salinger. I consider myself a huge fan of the man's work. *The Catcher in the Rye*, as I noted earlier, was crucial in my development into a compassionate human being. What I could not do in this book is cling to the narrative that seems to prevail in most discussions and presentations of the author and his work, most often *The Catcher in the Rye*, that the amazingly gifted author wrote a great novel by and large informed by soul-crushing war experiences and emerged too broken to deal with a rabid public that would not or could not leave him alone. Nor could I further advance the narrative that Salinger's interest in children reflected in his work was merely an instantiation of his lost innocence at the hands of the Nazis and his longing to recapture it. The facts simply do not allow it.

My conclusions are that Salinger's war experiences especially in relation to his Jewishness caused him to lash out at the pervasive white supremacy and white power structure that dominated American life through his protagonist Holden Caulfield. Stories such as "Blue Melody" and "Down at the Dinghy" evidence that Salinger was more than simply aware of racial forces at play in American culture. Further, Holden's preoccupation with sex, especially nonnormative sexualities, reflect Salinger's taboo sexual desire for very young girls, which he feared marked him as a deviant and drove him to seek out alternative religions that stressed sexual restraint. His compulsion for young girls overrode his distaste for macho aggressiveness and explains Holden's vacillation between macho behavior and criticism of same. Salinger's pursuit of young women right at the cusp of puberty explains more than anything else his rejection of the public and the press, his reclusivity, and his refusal to publish after 1965. He simply feared that his freedom would be taken away. This fear cost the world great work and individually devastated the careers of writers such as Ian Hamilton. The legacy of Salinger is not one befitting a great writer. Rather, Salinger's legacy is that of a man on the lam, fearful for his life, and violently protective of his freedom. I would agree that his estrangement from the public had a legitimizing effect on his work, casting it in a sort of somber light that ultimately appealed to borderline personalities like Chapman, Hinckley, and Bardo, who saw in the work and in the man an almost religious ideal that melded celebrity and nobility. All of these plot strands continue to fascinate fans, writers, and artists all over the world. Who was Salinger and how on earth did he write such a killer book and why on earth did he not write another one? This book attempts to meet this fascination halfway. I do not think Salinger should get a free pass because of one great novel. Nor do I think he should be ignored because of his weaknesses and flaws. Like a lot of writers, his best days seem to be when he was writing. I often say that I am my best self when I am reading and writing. My values and principles somehow are most present when I am engaged in reading and writing, but like Holden says of the so-called perverts on the other side of the hotel: they may be perverts, but I can be pretty crummy, too.

NOTES

INTRODUCTION

1. Julie Rivkin and Michael Ryan, "Introduction: The Politics of Culture," in *Literary Theory: An Anthology*, ed. Julie Rivkin and Michael Ryan (Malden, Mass.: Blackwell, 2004), 1233.

1. THE BIRTH OF A NOVEL

1. David Shields and Shane Salerno, *Salinger* (New York: Simon & Schuster, 2013), 158.

2. Shields and Salerno, *Salinger*, 158.

3. Kenneth Slawenski, *J. D. Salinger: A Life* (New York: Random House, 2010), 13.

4. "Famous Dropout J. D. Salinger Still Creates Mystique at College in Pennsylvania," *Fredericton (New Brunswick) Daily Gleaner*, September 9, 2013, A-A12.

5. Shields and Salerno, *Salinger*, 250.

6. Matthew Frye Jacobson, *Whiteness of a Different Color* (Cambridge, Mass.: Harvard University Press, 1998), 187.

7. Shelley Fisher Fishkin, "Interrogating 'Whiteness', Complicating 'Blackness': Remapping American Culture," *American Quarterly* 47, no. 3 (September 1995): 436.

8. Shields and Salerno, *Salinger*, 164.

9. Shields and Salerno, *Salinger*, 31.

10. Shelley Fisher Fishkin, *Was Huck Black? Mark Twain and African American Voices* (Oxford: Oxford University Press, 1994), 4.

11. Donald Janson, "Use of Salinger's *Catcher in the Rye* in Salem County School Stirs Dispute," *New York Times*, October 31, 1977, 67.

12. Donald Janson, "Help of Fundamentalist Minister Sought to Ban *Catcher in the Rye*," *New York Times*, November 9, 1977, 73.

13. Shields and Salerno, *Salinger*, 68.

14. Shields and Salerno, *Salinger*, 113.

15. Shields and Salerno, *Salinger*, 70.

16. Shields and Salerno, *Salinger*, 562.

17. Bruce Rind and Richard Yuill, "Hebephilia as Mental Disorder? A Historical, Cross-Cultural, Sociological, Cross-Species, Non-clinical Empirical, and Evolutionary Review," *Archives of Sexual Behavior* 41 (2012): 797.

18. Shields and Salerno, *Salinger*, 219–42.

19. Maxwell Strachan, "Reported Rapes Go Through the Roof on Game Day at Big Football Schools," Huffpost Sports, January 3, 2016, http://www.huffingtonpost.com/entry/college-football-rape_us_5685a429e4b014efe0da7ae0 (accessed May 22, 2016).

20. Michael S. Kimmel, "Masculinity as Homophobia: Fear, Shame, and Silence in the Construction of Gender Identity," in *Feminism and Masculinities*, ed. Peter F. Murphy (Oxford: Oxford University Press, 2004), 189.

21. Kimmel, "Masculinity as Homophobia," 185.

22. Georg Lukacs, "The Ideology of Modernism," in *Marxist Literary Theory*, ed. Terry Eagleton and Drew Milne (Malden, Mass.: Blackwell, 1966), 151.

2. *CATCHER* IN THE FIFTIES

1. Paul Alexander, *Salinger: A Biography* (Los Angeles: Renaissance Books, 1999), 137–38.

2. Peter Guralnick, *Last Train to Memphis: The Rise of Elvis Presley* (New York: Little, Brown, 1994), 44.

3. Guralnick, *Last Train to Memphis*, 28.

4. Guralnick, *Last Train to Memphis*, 43.

5. Guralnick, *Last Train to Memphis*, 44.

6. Guralnick, *Last Train to Memphis*, 64.

7. Guralnick, *Last Train to Memphis*, 75.

8. David Roediger, *Colored White: Transcending the Racial Past* (Berkeley: University of California Press, 2002), 216.

9. Kenneth Slawenski, *J. D. Salinger: A Life* (New York: Random House, 2010), 219.

10. Alexander, *Salinger*, 192.

11. Slawenski, *J. D. Salinger*, 217.

12. Roediger, *Transcending the Racial Past*, 215.

13. Pamela Hunt Steinle, *In Cold Fear:* The Catcher in the Rye *Censorship Controversies and Postwar American Character* (Columbus: Ohio State University Press, 2002), 15.

14. Anne L. Goodman, "Mad about Children," in *Critical Essays on Salinger's* The Catcher in the Rye, ed. Joel Salzberg (Boston: Hall, 1990), 23.

15. Anonymous, review of *The Catcher in the Rye*, in Salzberg, *Critical Essays*, 31.

16. Ernest Jones, "Case History of All of Us," in Salzberg, *Critical Essays*, 25.

17. Joel Salzberg, introduction, in Salzberg, *Critical Essays*, 7.

18. T. Morris Longstreth, review of *The Catcher in the Rye*, in Salzberg, *Critical Essays*, 31.

19. Arthur Heiserman and James E. Miller Jr., "J. D. Salinger: Some Crazy Cliff," in Salzberg, *Critical Essays*, 33.

20. Heiserman and Miller, "J. D. Salinger: Some Crazy Cliff," 35.

21. Heiserman and Miller, "J. D. Salinger: Some Crazy Cliff," 38.

22. David Shields and Shane Salerno, *Salinger* (New York: Simon & Schuster, 2013), 261.

23. Shields and Salerno, *Salinger*, 260.

3. *CATCHER* IN THE SIXTIES

1. Paul Alexander, *Salinger: A Biography* (Los Angeles: Renaissance Books, 1999), 210.

2. Kenneth Slawenski, *J. D. Salinger: A Life* (New York: Random House, 2010), 354.

3. Slawenski, *J. D. Salinger*, 356.

4. Harry Hansen, "Everybody Gets into Act but Elusive Mr. Salinger," *Chicago Tribune*, August 21, 1961, D6.

5. Slawenski, *J. D. Salinger*, 356.

6. Todd Gitlin, *The Sixties: Years of Hope, Days of Rage* (New York: Bantam, 1987), 406.

7. Ethan A. Russell with Gerard Van Der Leun, *Let It Bleed: The Rolling Stones, Altamont, and the End of the Sixties* (New York: Springboard, 2009), xv.

8. Russell, *Let It Bleed*, xiv.

9. Russell, *Let It Bleed*, 62.

10. Russell, *Let it Bleed*, 188.

11. Russell, *Let It Bleed*, 188.

12. Russell, *Let It Bleed*, 198.

13. David Shields and Shane Salerno, *Salinger* (New York: Simon & Schuster, 2013), 352.

14. Shields and Salerno, *Salinger*, 354.

15. Pamela Hunt Steinle, *In Cold Fear:* The Catcher in the Rye *Censorship Controversies and Postwar American Character* (Columbus: Ohio State University Press, 2002), 15.

16. Steinle, *In Cold Fear*, 61.

17. Eve Kosofsky Sedgwick, *Epistemology of the Closet* (Berkeley: University of California Press, 1990), 72.

18. "FBI Says It Has No File on *Catcher in the Rye* Author J. D. Salinger," *Toronto Star*, March 1, 2010, 1.

4. CATCHER IN THE SEVENTIES

1. *The Black Power Mixtape*, documentary, directed by Göran Olsson (MPI Home Video, 2011).

2. Paul Alexander, *Salinger: A Biography* (Los Angeles: Renaissance Books, 1999), 242.

3. Alexander, *Salinger*, 244.

4. Alexander, *Salinger*, 246.

5. Kenneth Slawenski, *J. D. Salinger: A Life* (New York: Random House, 2010), 380.

6. Slawenski, *J. D. Salinger*, 381.

7. "Special Campus Reading Issue," *Chicago Tribune*, May 19, 1974, E26A.

8. *The Black Power Mixtape*.

9. *The Black Power Mixtape*.

10. Heather Ann Thompson, *Blood in the Water: The Attica Prison Uprising of 1971 and Its Legacy* (New York: Pantheon, 2016), 111.

11. Thompson, *Blood in the Water*, 109.

12. Thompson, *Blood in the Water*, 147.

13. Thompson, *Blood in the Water*, 192.

14. Alexander, *Salinger*, 254–55.

15. Alexander, *Salinger*, 259–63.

16. Helen Dudar, "In Search of J. D. Salinger, Publishing's Invisible Man," *Chicago Tribune*, June 19, 1979, A1.

17. Ron Rosenbaum, "Sex in the Salinger Archives? A Little-Known Short Story Might Be a Clue," *Slate Magazine*, February 4, 2010, http://www.slate.com/articles/life/the_spectator/2010/02/sex_in_the_salinger_archives.html.

18. Pamela Hunt Steinle, *In Cold Fear:* The Catcher in the Rye *Censorship Controversies and Postwar American Character* (Columbus: Ohio State University Press, 2002), 68.

5. CATCHER IN THE EIGHTIES

1. David Shields and Shane Salerno, *Salinger* (New York: Simon & Schuster, 2013), 498.

2. "25 'Must Read' Books for Students," *Chicago Tribune*, November 18, 1984, C4.

3. David Margolick, "Whose Words Are They Anyway," *New York Times*, November 1, 1987, BR1.

4. Mordecai Richler, "Rises at Dawn, Writes, Then Retires," *New York Times*, June 5, 1988, BR7.

5. David Toop, *Rap Attack 3* (London: Serpent's Tail, 2000), 173.

6. Toop, *Rap Attack*, 209–10.

7. Adam Gopnik, "The Caging of America," *New Yorker*, January 30, 2012, 72.

8. Tricia Rose, *Black Noise: Rap Music and Black Culture in Contemporary America* (Middletown, Conn.: Wesleyan University Press, 1994), 11–12.

9. Pamela Hunt Steinle, *In Cold Fear:* The Catcher in the Rye *Censorship Controversies and Postwar American Character* (Columbus: Ohio State University Press, 2002), 2.

10. Steinle, *In Cold Fear*, 89.

11. David Foster Wallace, *A Supposedly Fun Thing I'll Never Do Again* (London: Abacus, 2013), 22.

12. Shields and Salerno, *Salinger*, 232.

13. Shields and Salerno, *Salinger*, 255.

14. Alison Alexander, Louise M. Benjamin, Keisha Hoerrner, and Darrell Roe, "'We'll Be Back in a Moment': A Content Analysis of Advertisements in Children's Television in the 1950s," *Journal of Advertising* 27, no. 3, Advertising to Children (Autumn 1998): 1–2.

15. Morris Dickstein, *Leopards in the Temple: The Transformation of American Fiction: 1945–1970* (Cambridge, Mass.: Harvard University Press, 2002), 7.

16. Shields and Salerno, *Salinger*, 433.

17. Shields and Salerno, *Salinger*, 427.

18. Shields and Salerno, *Salinger*, 82.

19. Shields and Salerno, *Salinger*, 38.

20. Shields and Salerno, *Salinger*, 65.

21. Shields and Salerno, *Salinger*, 87.

22. Wallace, *A Supposedly Fun Thing*, 25.

23. Shields and Salerno, *Salinger*, 493.

24. Shields and Salerno, *Salinger*, 505–6.

25. Wallace, *A Supposedly Fun Thing*, 26.

26. Shields and Salerno, *Salinger*, 463.

27. "A Real Nowhere Man: Profile of Lennon's Killer Jobless Hawaii 'Wacko' Put under Suicide Watch," *Los Angeles Times*, December 9, 1980, A1.

28. George Getschow and Brenton R. Schlender, "Family Portrait: Friends View Parents of Hinckley as Loving, Devoted to Children," *Wall Street Journal*, April 6, 1981, 1.

29. Shields and Salerno, *Salinger*, 482.

30. Stephen Braun and Charisse Jones, "Actress' Bright Success Collided with Obsession," *Los Angeles Times*, July 23, 1989, A1.

31. Shields and Salerno, *Salinger*, 485.

6. *CATCHER* IN THE NINETIES
TO THE PRESENT

1. Michael Eric Dyson, *The Black Presidency: Barack Obama and the Politics of Race in America* (New York: Houghton Mifflin Harcourt, 2016), xv.

2. Jonathan Chait, "Bill Clinton, O. J. Simpson, Clarence Thomas, and the Politics of 1990s Racial Backlash," *National Interest*, July 4, 2016, http://nymag.com/daily/intelligencer/2016/06/clinton-and-the-politics-of-90s-racial-backlash.html (accessed August 3, 2016).

3. "The 100 Most Frequently Challenged Books of 1990–99," *Lincoln Journal Star*, September 25, 2000, C3.

4. "Gatsby Is Top Literary Character, Panel Says," *New York Times*, March 9, 2002, 18.

5. David Shields and Shane Salerno, *Salinger* (New York: Simon & Schuster, 2013), 511.

6. Kenneth Slawenski, *J. D. Salinger: A Life* (New York: Random House, 2010), 395.

7. Slawenski, *J. D. Salinger*, 395.

8. John Blake, "What Black America Won't Miss about Obama," CNN, July 1, 2016, http://www.cnn.com/2016/06/30/politics/why-black-america-may-be-relieved-to-see-obama-go/index.html (accessed August 3, 2016).

9. Slawenski, *J. D. Salinger*, 401.

10. Slawenski, *J. D. Salinger*, 404–6.

11. Philip Marchand, "They Had a Grudge against Adulthood; Michael Jackson as an American Man-Child," *National Post*, July 11, 2009, WP11.

12. Shields and Salerno, *Salinger*, 550–51.

13. Bart Barnes, "After *Catcher in the Rye*, Writer Became Famed Recluse," *Washington Post*, January 29, 2010, A01.

14. Charles McGrath, "J. D. Salinger, Reclusive American Author, 91; Obituary," *International Herald Tribune*, January 30, 2010, 4.

15. Shields and Salerno, *Salinger*, 574–75.

16. Joyce Maynard, "Was Salinger Too Pure for This World?" *New York Times*, September 15, 2013, SR9.

17. Howard Kissel, "No Cause for Re-Joyceing Maynard Looks Back, Yet Again—This Time at Her Life and Some Time with J. D. Salinger," *New York Daily News*, September 13, 1998, 24.

18. Jonathan Yardley, "Lecher in the Rye? Hardly," *Washington Post*, May 17, 1999, C2.

19. Jessica Rizzo, "Catch as Catch Can: *Holden* at the New Ohio Theatre," *Theater Times*, January 9, 2017.

20. Anisa George, *Holden*, performed at FringeArts Philadelphia, October 2015.

21. Guy Lodge, "Sundance Film Review: *Rebel in the Rye*," *Variety*, January 25, 2017, http://variety.com/2017/film/markets-festivals/rebel-in-the-rye-review-1201969671/ .

22. Jordan Hoffman, "*Rebel in the Rye* Review—J. D. Salinger Drama Catches Attention but Sinks into Cliché," *Guardian*, January 25, 2017, https://www.theguardian.com/film/2017/jan/25/rebel-in-the-rye-review-jd-salinger-nicholas-hoult .

23. John DeFore, "*Rebel in the Rye*: Film Review; Sundance 2017," *Hollywood Reporter*, January 25, 2017, http://www.hollywoodreporter.com/review/rebel-rye-review-968339 .

CONCLUSION

1. David Shields and Shane Salerno, *Salinger* (New York: Simon & Schuster, 2013), 68.

2. Kenneth Holm, responses to *The Catcher in the Rye*, University of Wisconsin, Parkside, 2015.

3. Michael Jensen, responses to *The Catcher in the Rye*, University of Wisconsin, Parkside, 2015.

4. Aleu Govani, responses to *The Catcher in the Rye*, Brown Deer High School, 2016.

5. Peter Her, responses to *The Catcher in the Rye*. Brown Deer High School, 2016.

6. Molly Olk, responses to *The Catcher in the Rye*, Brown Deer High School, 2016.

7. Michael S. Kimmel, "Masculinity as Homophobia: Fear, Shame, and Silence in the Construction of Gender Identity," in *Feminism and Masculinities*, ed. Peter F. Murphy (Oxford: Oxford University Press, 2004), 192.

8. Steve Martinot, *Machinery of Whiteness: Studies in the Structure of Racialization* (Philadelphia: Temple University Press, 2010), 19.

9. Martinot, *Machinery*, 14.

10. Jennifer Agiesta, "2016: Last Call for Working Class Whites?" CNN Politics, September 21, 2016, http://www.cnn.com/2016/09/20/politics/2016-election-white-working-class-voters/index.html (accessed September 26, 2016).

11. Agiesta, "2016."

12. Agiesta, "2016."

REFERENCES

Agiesta, Jennifer. "2016: Last Call for Working Class Whites?" CNN Politics. September 21, 2016. http://www.cnn.com/2016/09/20/politics/2016-election-white-working-class-voters/index.html. Accessed September 26, 2016.

Alexander, Alison, Louise M. Benjamin, Keisha Hoerrner, and Darrell Roe. "'We'll Be Back in a Moment': A Content Analysis of Advertisements in Children's Television in the 1950s." *Journal of Advertising* 27, no. 3, Advertising to Children (Autumn 1998): 1–9.

Alexander, Paul. *Salinger: A Biography.* Los Angeles: Renaissance Books, 1999.

Anonymous. Review of *The Catcher in the Rye*. In *Critical Essays on Salinger's* The Catcher in the Rye, edited by Joel Salzberg, 31. Boston: Hall, 1990.

Barnes, Bart. "After *Catcher in the Rye*, Writer Became Famed Recluse." *Washington Post*, January 29, 2010, A01.

The Black Power Mixtape. Documentary. Directed by Göran Olsson. MPI Home Video, 2011.

Blake, John. "What Black America Won't Miss about Obama." CNN. July 1, 2016. http://www.cnn.com/2016/06/30/politics/why-black-america-may-be-relieved-to-see-obama-go/index.html. Accessed August 3, 2016.

Braun, Stephen, and Charisse Jones. "Actress' Bright Success Collided with Obsession." *Los Angeles Times*, July 23, 1989, A1.

Chait, Jonathan. "Bill Clinton, O. J. Simpson, Clarence Thomas, and the Politics of 1990s Racial Backlash." *National Interest*, July 4, 2016. http://nymag.com/daily/intelligencer/2016/06/clinton-and-the-politics-of-90s-racial-backlash.html. Accessed August 3, 2016.

Chicago Tribune. "Special Campus Reading Issue." May 19, 1974, E26A.

———. "25 'Must Read' Books for Students." November 18, 1984, C4.

DeFore, John. "*Rebel in the Rye*: Film Review; Sundance 2017." *Hollywood Reporter*, January 25, 2017. http://www.hollywoodreporter.com/review/rebel-rye-review-968339.

Dickstein, Morris. *Leopards in the Temple: The Transformation of American Fiction; 1945–1970*. Cambridge, Mass.: Harvard University Press, 2002.

Dudar, Helen. "In Search of J. D. Salinger, Publishing's Invisible Man." *Chicago Tribune*, June 19, 1979, A1.

Dyson, Michael Eric. *The Black Presidency: Barack Obama and the Politics of Race in America*. New York: Houghton Mifflin Harcourt, 2016.

Fishkin, Shelley Fisher. "Interrogating 'Whiteness,' Complicating 'Blackness': Remapping American Culture." *American Quarterly* 47, no. 3 (September 1995): 428–66.

———. *Was Huck Black? Mark Twain and African American Voices*. Oxford: Oxford University Press, 1994.

Fredericton (New Brunswick) Daily Gleaner. "Famous Dropout J. D. Salinger Still Creates Mystique at College in Pennsylvania." September 9, 2013, A-A12.

George, Anisa. *Holden*. Performed at FringeArts Philadelphia, October 2015.

Getschow, George, and Brenton R. Schlender. "Family Portrait: Friends View Parents of Hinckley as Loving, Devoted to Children." *Wall Street Journal*, April 6, 1981, 1.

Gitlin, Todd. *The Sixties: Years of Hope, Days of Rage*. New York: Bantam, 1987.

Goodman, Anne L. "Mad about Children." In *Critical Essays on Salinger's* The Catcher in the Rye, edited by Joel Salzberg, 23–24. Boston: Hall, 1990.

Gopnik, Adam. "The Caging of America." *New Yorker*, January 30, 2012, 72.

Govani, Aleu. Responses to *The Catcher in the Rye*. Brown Deer High School. 2016.

Guralnick, Peter. *Last Train to Memphis: The Rise of Elvis Presley*. New York: Little, Brown, 1994.

Hansen, Harry. "Everybody Gets into Act but Elusive Mr. Salinger." *Chicago Tribune*, August 21, 1961, D6.

Heiserman, Arthur, and James E. Miller Jr. "J. D. Salinger: Some Crazy Cliff." In *Critical Essays on Salinger's* The Catcher in the Rye, edited by Joel Salzberg, 32–39. Boston: Hall, 1990.

Her, Peter. Responses to *The Catcher in the Rye*. Brown Deer High School. 2016.

Hoffman, Jordan. *"Rebel in the Rye* Review—J. D. Salinger Drama Catches Attention but Sinks into Cliché." *Guardian*, January 25, 2017. https://www.theguardian.com/film/2017/jan/25/rebel-in-the-rye-review-jd-salinger-nicholas-hoult.

Holm, Kenneth. Responses to *The Catcher in the Rye*. University of Wisconsin, Parkside. 2015.

Jacobson, Matthew Frye. *Whiteness of a Different Color*. Cambridge, Mass.: Harvard University Press, 1998.

Janson, Donald. "Help of Fundamentalist Minister Sought to Ban *Catcher in the Rye*." *New York Times*, November 9, 1977, 73.

———. "Use of Salinger's *Catcher in the Rye* in Salem County School Stirs Dispute." *New York Times*, October 31, 1977, 67.

Jensen, Michael. Responses to *The Catcher in the Rye*. University of Wisconsin, Parkside. 2015.

Jones, Ernest. "Case History of All of Us." In *Critical Essays on Salinger's* The Catcher in the Rye, edited by Joel Salzberg ,24–25. Boston: Hall, 1990.

Kimmel, Michael S. "Masculinity as Homophobia: Fear, Shame, and Silence in the Construction of Gender Identity." In *Feminism and Masculinities*, edited by Peter F. Murphy, 182–99. Oxford: Oxford University Press, 2004.

Kissel, Howard. "No Cause for Re-Joyceing Maynard Looks Back, Yet Again—This Time at Her Life and Some Time with J. D. Salinger." *New York Daily News*, September 13, 1998, 24.

Lincoln Journal Star. "The 100 Most Frequently Challenged Books of 1990–99." September 25, 2000, C3.

Lodge, Guy. "Sundance Film Review: *Rebel in the Rye*." *Variety*. January 25, 2017. http://variety.com/2017/film/markets-festivals/rebel-in-the-rye-review-1201969671/.

Longstreth, T. Morris. Review of *The Catcher in the Rye*. In *Critical Essays on Salinger's* The Catcher in the Rye, edited by Joel Salzberg, 30–31. Boston: Hall, 1990.

Los Angeles Times. "A Real Nowhere Man: Profile of Lennon's Killer Jobless Hawaii 'Wacko' Put under Suicide Watch." December 9, 1980, A1.

Lukacs, Georg. "The Ideology of Modernism." In *Marxist Literary Theory*, edited by Terry Eagleton and Drew Milne, 141–62. Malden, Mass.: Blackwell, 1966.

Marchand, Philip. "They Had a Grudge against Adulthood; Michael Jackson as an American Man-Child." *National Post*, July 11, 2009, WP11.

Margolick, David. "Whose Words Are They Anyway." *New York Times*, November 1, 1987, BR1.

Martinot, Steve. *Machinery of Whiteness: Studies in the Structure of Racialization*. Philadelphia: Temple University Press, 2010.

Maynard, Joyce. "Was Salinger Too Pure for This World?" *New York Times*, September 15, 2013, SR9.

McGrath, Charles. "J. D. Salinger, Reclusive American Author, 91; Obituary." *International Herald Tribune*, January 30, 2010, 4.

New York Times. "Gatsby Is Top Literary Character, Panel Says." March 9, 2002, 18.

Olk, Molly. Responses to *The Catcher in the Rye*. Brown Deer High School. 2016.

Richler, Mordecai. "Rises at Dawn, Writes, Then Retires." *New York Times*, June 5, 1988, BR7.

Rind, Bruce, and Richard Yuill. "Hebephilia as Mental Disorder? A Historical, Cross-Cultural, Sociological, Cross-Species, Non-Clinical Empirical, and Evolutionary Review." *Archives of Sexual Behavior* 41 (2012): 797–829.

Rivkin, Julie, and Michael Ryan. "Introduction: The Politics of Culture." In *Literary Theory: An Anthology*, edited by Julie Rivkin and Michael Ryan, 1233–34. Malden, Mass.: Blackwell, 2004.

Rizzo, Jessica. "Catch as Catch Can: *Holden* at the New Ohio Theatre." *Theater Times*, January 9, 2017.

Roediger, David. *Colored White: Transcending the Racial Past*. Berkeley: University of California Press, 2002.

Rose, Tricia. *Black Noise: Rap Music and Black Culture in Contemporary America*. Middletown, Conn.: Wesleyan University Press, 1994.

Rosenbaum, Ron. "Sex in the Salinger Archives? A Little-Known Short Story Might Be a Clue." *Slate Magazine*, February 4, 2010. http://www.slate.com/articles/life/the_spectator/2010/02/sex_in_the_salinger_archives.html.

Russell, Ethan A., with Gerard Van Der Leun. *Let It Bleed: The Rolling Stones, Altamont, and the End of the Sixties*. New York: Springboard, 2009.

Salzberg, Joel, ed. *Critical Essays on Salinger's* The Catcher in the Rye. Boston: Hall, 1990.

Salzberg, Joel. Introduction. In *Critical Essays on Salinger's* The Catcher in the Rye, edited by Joel Salzberg, 1–22. Boston: Hall, 1990.

Sedgwick, Eve Kosofsky. *Epistemology of the Closet*. Berkeley: University of California Press, 1990.

Shields, David, and Shane Salerno. *Salinger*. New York: Simon & Schuster, 2013.

Slawenski, Kenneth. *J. D. Salinger: A Life*. New York: Random House, 2010.

Steinle, Pamela Hunt. *In Cold Fear:* The Catcher in the Rye *Censorship Controversies and Postwar American Character*. Columbus: Ohio State University Press, 2002.

Strachan, Maxwell. "Reported Rapes Go Through the Roof on Game Day at Big Football Schools." Huffpost Sports. January 3. 2016. http://www.huffingtonpost.com/entry/college-football-rape_us_5685a429e4b014efe0da7ae0. Accessed May 22, 2016.

Thompson, Heather Ann. *Blood in the Water: The Attica Prison Uprising of 1971 and Its Legacy*. New York: Pantheon, 2016.

Toop, David. *Rap Attack 3*. London: Serpent's Tail, 2000.

Toronto Star. "FBI Says It Has No File on *Catcher in the Rye* Author J. D. Salinger." March 1, 2010, 1.

Wallace, David Foster. *A Supposedly Fun Thing I'll Never Do Again*. London: Abacus, 2013.

Yardley, Jonathan. "Lecher in the Rye? Hardly." *Washington Post*, May 17, 1999, C2.

INDEX

ABOUT THE AUTHOR

Josef Benson is assistant professor of English at the University of Wisconsin, Parkside, and author of *Hypermasculinities in the Contemporary Novel: Cormac McCarthy, Toni Morrison, and James Baldwin* (Rowman & Littlefield 2014). Additionally, his work has appeared in more than twenty publications, including *Journal of Medical Humanities*, *Journal of Bisexuality*, and *Southwestern American Literature*.

Lightning Source UK Ltd.
Milton Keynes UK
UKHW041339231221
396139UK00001B/33